Lucky Break

How I Became a Writer

edited by
Howard Junker

Heinemann
Portsmouth, NH

Heinemann
A division of Reed Elsevier Inc.
361 Hanover Street
Portsmouth, NH 03801-3912

http://www.heinemann.com

We would like to thank those who have given their permission
to include material in this book:

Bill Berkson's "The Beginner" is a modified version of excerpts
from the entry "Bill Berkson /1939–" in *Gale Contemporary
Authors Autobiography Series,* Volume 31, by Gale Research
Publications. Copyright ©1999 Bill Berkson.

Dorianne Laux's "Girl Poet" is adapted from a talk given at
Lewis-Clark College, Idaho, for Women's History Month,
March, 1998.

The essays by Opal Palmer Adisa, Sheila Ballantyne, Bill Berkson, Forrest Hamer, Adam Hochschild, Ginu Kamani, Philip
Levine, Aleida Rodríguez, Kay Ryan, Octavio Solis, Sallie Tisdale, and David Rains Wallace first appeared in *ZYZZYVA,* a
journal of West Coast writers and artists, and are reprinted with
permission of the authors.

The editor is greatful for grants from the Wallace Alexander Ger-
bode Foundation and the Zellerbach Family Fund in support of
this project.

Cataloging-In-Publication data is on file
at the Library of Congress
ISBN: 0-325-00156-1

Editor: Lisa A. Barnett
Manufacturing: Louise Richardson

Printed in the United States of America on acid-free paper

02 01 00 99 MV 1 2 3 4

CONTENTS

INTRODUCTION

I stole the title for this collection from my daughter's favorite author, Roald Dahl. It appears in a collection of his short stories, *The Wonderful Story of Henry Sugar and Six More,* and it is not at all out of place, because Dahl conceives of his *bildungsroman* as a fabulous story: He became a writer because of a lucky break! What was most fabulous about this break, he admits, is that "in this century . . . just about every single writer who has finally become successful . . . has started out in some other job. . . ."

Dahl was describing, of course, the trajectory of writers before the triumph of writers' workshops, before the Master of Fine Arts in Creative Writing came to be seen as a "terminal degree," that is, a potential meal ticket. In the old days, Dahl knew, writers cut their teeth on journalism, advertising, or some other sub-literary genre; he includes teaching, medicine, and the law as other potential starter careers. No one learned to write in a classroom; you taught yourself the craft as best you could, by imitation, if not else, and you did so not in a privileged circumstance, but in the midst of an on-going life.

Dahl, nonetheless, does trace his vocational trail back to his schooldays, specifically, back to the formative experience of being beaten as a schoolboy. How being brutalized as an eight-year-old helped Dahl become a writer he does not explain, but it goes without saying that almost no one becomes a writer who has not suffered, who does not long to construct an alternative history, to repair past damages, either with a vengeance or not.

An early experience with deprivation and oppression (and even with evil) may be necessary, Dahl suggests, but it is not sufficient. To his suffering, his schooldays also added inspiration, in the form of the Saturday morning lectures given by the "blessed beautiful Mrs. O'Connor with her whacky clothes and her grey hair flying in all directions." It was her task to keep a study hall filled with a hundred pre-teen boys supervised until lunch, until, that is, the masters had returned from the pub. And she did so with fervent talks about the One Hundred Landmarks of English Literature. "What marvelous exciting fun it was!" Dahl recalls. Yes, *fun,* the essential feeling with which every writer should begin: a passionate involvement with the writers of the past, a love affair with literature.

Dahl's actual lucky break came during World War II. A fighter pilot, he was shot down in North Africa—no, that was not his lucky break—and, after he recovered and flew several more perilous missions, he was assigned to the British Embassy in Washington as an assistant air attaché—no, that was still not his lucky break. His third day on duty, C. S. Forester, "the best teller of tales about the sea since Joseph Conrad," walked into his office and asked for an interview: Wouldn't an account of Dahl's wartime adventures interest readers of the *Saturday Evening Post* and arouse their support for the defense of Britain?

Forester did not make much of an attempt to do an interview over lunch, but, since both men enjoyed their food and wine and their conversation, Dahl did feel some sense of obligation. Over coffee, he apologized for not having supplied much material. He offered to go home that night and type up some notes; perhaps these would help Forester write his for-the-war-effort article. Two weeks later Forester sent Dahl a letter with a check for $900—the *Post* had decided to publish Dahl's notes!

So it was as easy as that. (Forester even set Dahl up with his own agent!) And it may still be that easy to become a writer, granted talent, inspiration, hard work, and so on.

In this collection, nineteen contemporary writers tell nineteen different stories. Some, like Blair Fuller and Peter Booth Wiley, suggest there was a genetic element involved, the born-poet syndrome. Others, like Bill Berkson and Justin Chin, feel they had to break away, to renounce their patrimony, in order to find the space and freedom to write. Some, like Jewelle Gomez and Forrest Hamer, had their subject matter in mind long before they could imagine the possibility of putting it all into words. Others, taking Dahl one step further, claim it really was just an accident, however happy, that pointed them in the right direction: Ginu Kamani goes so far as to suggest that her creative spirits were first nurtured by disco music, strange as that may seem. And, staking a claim for the great guild tradition of the apprentice and the master—what's lately called mentoring, Philip Levine details his arduous passage as a graduate student at Stanford, working under the stern critic/poet Yvor Winters.

In the end, of course, becoming a writer is the least of it. Hard as it might be to get published the first time—if that's what it means to *become* a writer—*being* a writer, making one's life as a writer—is even harder. But perhaps that story, well beyond the territory of lucky breaks, should be the subject of another volume. □

Howard Junker

LYING IN THE TALL GRASSES, EATING CANE

Opal Palmer Adisa

*T*he first stories I wrote were all composed while I lay nestled in the tall grasses, peeling away the sharp skin of the cane with my teeth and feeling deep pleasure as the sweet, sticky juice trickled down my cheeks onto my neck. I would stay concealed by the tall grasses for hours, gazing up at the clouds, observing the shapes of cows, birds, one animal after another dissolving and transforming into another. The heat of the sun penetrated my skin, and the chalky, gauze-like clouds dazzled my eyes, and words as liquid as cane juice, as comforting as the tall grasses, came to me.

When I turned eight years old, I started to compose stories and poems on paper, but I never shared them with anyone. I was just beginning my dance with words; they were as sweet and sensual as the chocolate bars I held in my mouth until they melted, gluing my tongue to the roof of my mouth and leaving my fingers stained a sticky brown. Writing was just for me; it was my secret, like my favorite places to go off to be alone. I often wandered aimlessly over my community with its immense space dotted with large cotton trees, tenanted by acres and acres of cane and banana fields, many connecting canals and dense forest where numerous species of lizards, birds, and other critters dwelled. I recorded almost all I saw and stored the rest in my memory. I felt an urgency and deep need to do this. Mostly, I felt the people around me did not perceive their own immense beauty and truth.

Almost every Sunday my family went to the beach. There I would pass hours splashing in the water, lying by the shore allowing the ebb and flow of the waves to wash over me, building sand castles, rubbing sand all over my body, and listening intently to the chatter of the ocean. The first poem I had published, at thirteen, was entitled "The Sounds I Like to Hear." The roar and caw of the sea was the dominant image. However, the abundant glee of the wind rustling through trees, flapping clothes on lines, swirling dust into the air, and awakening my skin, also resonated throughout the poem. I was attracted to sounds—mosquitoes buzzing, lizards croaking, and dogs yapping in rounds at night. Colors mesmerized me—verdant mountain ranges perched against aqua skies, purple-hued skin touched off by an indigo shirt, a cinnamon-toned face regaled in a golden hat.

Movements caught hold of my breath—the gait of youths on their way to a soccer match, market women balancing huge baskets on their heads, cane cutters dancing with the swing of their machetes. I was also enthralled by the deep, full laughter of people and the way they fervently clung to their beliefs. I always nestled in some corner, being seen and not heard, taking in the talk of the "big" people. I was greedy for their stories; my hunger was never satiated. The relationships between people fascinated me, but I was more intrigued by what was not said, gestures that belied words. I was drawn to the working class and their open display of emotions. The women were particularly dramatic. When angered or hurt, they would shout to attract an audience, their arms akimbo, their very stance daring the person who wronged them to step over the boundary they had defined. They often solicited fights to appease their wounded feelings. I always stood on the fringes, entranced, trying to make sense of such wanton displays of emotions. My middle-class mother was preaching just the opposite: restraint, quiet, lady-like behavior. Whereas the middle class appeared to suck in their pain until they became bitter, the working class was unabashed. I would often sneak off so I could be with them, to listen in on their conversation, to drink in their zest for life, to observe their every action. They lived life with a robust intensity that tingled me to the core. I searched my mind for words, language with which to convey the intensity of their feelings, but believed myself to be sadly lacking. So I stored their stories in the recesses of my mind.

But that did not make me a writer. I never thought of myself as a writer, I suppose as a result of being reared in a colonial society with a British education that vociferously denounced Jamaica's cultural ethos. In fact, we were presumed to lack history and therefore had nothing worthwhile to write about. I always suspected this history I was being taught was somehow erroneous or at best lopsided and suspect. I didn't feel wrong or inferior, yet my education was telling me that even the way we Jamaicans spoke was wrong. I remember my teachers drilling me to speak the Queen's English. All the books I read and the poems I memorized were by British or American poets, almost all of whom were men, and presumably dead. At that time, I truly believed that a writer was synonymous with death. One had to die to be a writer, and I was not prepared to die, even for the glory of seeing my words in print. More important, I believed only people who lived elsewhere, and who talked about sleet, which I could not imagine, and watched daffodils, were writers. I had not yet read Claude McKay's "The Tropics in New York" in which bananas, tangerines and mangoes, emblems of my culture, are mentioned, even elevated. Although my family boasted a large library, and my mother and sister were avid readers, I can say with perfect honesty that I never read a book or poem by a black person, from anywhere in the world, until I was sixteen and had moved to New York. There, while completing a year of high school, I was introduced to Langston Hughes, Gwendolyn Brooks, and Jean Toomer.

Toomer's *Cane* is the single text that is most responsible for me recognizing and answering the call of a writer. The title attracted me, and I was captured completely by Toomer's lyrical surrealism that transported me to a familiar terrain, reminiscent of the sugar estate on which my navel-string was buried. Like the Jamaica of my childhood, Toomer's *Cane* was inhabited by black people with their everyday extraordinary simplicity and grace. I knew in that moment, upon completing that volume, that I wanted to write, not in the surreptitious manner that I had been engaged in all along, but openly, to share with others.

Those African American writers led me to discover Caribbean and African writers when I entered Hunter College. I was amazed and also angry that it took me so long to discover these writers, many of whom were Jamaicans, and most of whom had been writing before I was born. Why did it take me eighteen years to discover them, and then so far from home? From then on, I read avidly, and tentatively began to seek out black writers in New York.

In my nineteenth year, two events set me firmly on my course to being a writer. First, I met LeRoy Clarke, a Trinidadian painter and poet. When I told him I wrote, he invited me to show him my work. He was surprised when the following week I handed him three folders with almost two hundred poems. Nonetheless, he took and read them. Then he called me up and declared that I was a poet. Clarke recommended that I rework some of the poems and suggested that I attend readings regularly. Second, I had the good fortune to hear Sonia Sanchez read. There before me was a black woman, as petite as me, spewing fiery words, resonating truth. Meeting Clarke and seeing Sanchez read launched my career. The fear I always harbored about sharing my work receded, and I found my voice reading at open mikes. I was amazed when people came up to me afterward and said they liked my poems and urged me to submit my work for publication.

By the time I returned to Jamaica six years later, armed with a B.A. degree, things had changed. Books by Caribbean writers were being taught in the schools, and the poetry scene was vibrant. I was fortunate to be mentored by Mervyn Morris and Kamau Brathwaite, who were teaching at the University of the West Indies, and whose love and guidance I still value. I wrote and hosted a poetry program on one of the radio stations that featured the works of published as well as unpublished writers. My poems were published almost weekly for three years in the Sunday literary section of one of the newspapers. I wrote feverishly. I continued to observe my people, and, with the shift in education, there was a shift in the importance of the Jamaican language. I began to experiment and incorporate my mother tongue into my work. I remembered the dialect poetry of Louise Bennett, which I had heard all throughout my childhood, and wondered why I had not before considered her poetry on equal footing with Longfellow's, for instance. Studying Bennett's work for the first time strengthened my resolve to incorporate the Jamaican language into my work, *me could labrish and write fi we yarns.*

I have been writing now for more than twenty years. I call myself a writer, but sometimes I question whether or not I am a full-fledged writer. I have written more poems than I can count or that will ever be published, and I have four books to my credit. But I have never given writing first priority. It is still what I do after I have done everything else, the last thing I get to after I have taken care of my children, cleaned my house, marked my students' papers, and answered numerous telephone calls. I have not given this long-standing, faithful lover, this passionate devotee, my full attention. In some respect, I still fear what might happen to the rest of my life if I were to abandon myself to this paramour. In many ways, I sense that the depth of my feelings borders on sickness; yet I am also painfully aware that this lover is as necessary as the blood that feeds my heart.

The memory of the grass tickling my skin, the sun pressing the clothes to my body, the sweetness of the cane juice in my mouth, and the clear blue skies peering down at me are still very vivid. These images, along with the vibrant energy of my people, continue to fuel my work, and I pray they will never abandon me. I cannot not write. I am still an apprentice, kneeling at the foot of this god.

> i didn't choose this lover
> it was not i who went
> in search of his ardor
> believe me
> i ignored him
> for as long as i could
> but he always shadowed me
>
> then one day
> when all the glow
> was sucked from the sun
> when tears were a brine
> on my cheeks
> he came to me
> not open
> like a friend
> offering comfort
> not stealthily
> like a desperate thief
> but like an animal
> tracking my smell
>
> i was vulnerable
> you must understand
> i needed to hear
> someone say
> i was special
> i needed to feel
> as if i was important
> worthy of someone's love

so i opened my arms
and he pressed his body
to my chest
blew sultry breath on my neck
caressed the muscles in my lower back
and his kisses
how to describe the confectionery
sweetness of his tongue
in my mouth
the soothing warmth
of his hands
caressing   luring
opening me up

i didn't want
this lover
truly
my affection had been unrequited
for many years
for i suspected
always knew
should i slip
should i allow this lover
to get hold of my hand
to gaze into my face
that i would never be able
to free myself from him
that he would forever
be in my bed
every word i speak
from there on
would only mouth his desires

it's dangerous
but wonderful
my work   this lover

i'm lost
christened writer
truly i am
to this suitor

i am a writer □

THANK YOU, LEONARD WOLF

Sheila Ballantyne

1959 I wrote poetry in my youth. There was a moment in time, one moment only, when I thought of myself as a poet. It was in San Francisco, on Grant Avenue in North Beach in the late fifties, in the Co-Existence Bagel Shop. I'd been hanging out with friends on a Saturday night and had fallen into a marijuana moment with a red-haired guy with eyes like pinwheels at the next table. He spoke first: "I'm a poet." I said, "I'm a poet too." We scribbled happily together on the butcher paper between us. The cafe was dense with smoke. Everyone was smoking: mostly Gauloises. I hadn't yet switched to Kents, but when I did, I knew I'd never go back to the Co-Existence. Kents were for the downtown girls, and I would be graduating next semester—to selling scarves in the Emporium basement. College was definitely over.

The following year yielded a new job: medical records. By the time I got married and had children, I knew my life was over with regard to art and literature. My last moment as a poet was when I stepped out of the Co-Existence Bagel Shop and had a heated altercation with a cop who'd been posted there just to apprehend people like me. He said, "Young lady, you'd better put your shoes on or I'll have you arrested." "I like my feet bare," I said, and began walking up Grant Avenue with all the smokers, drifters, and jazz boys on their way to a gig up the block, my sandals swinging loosely from my fingers. "I said, 'Put your shoes on or I'll put you under arrest.'" I believed in individual freedom then. This cop was out to grind poetry under his heel. By now, my friends were pulling me away from the action. It was a humiliating moment for all of us. I knew my life as a poet was over. And this was the defining moment.

1968 By now there were two babies tearing the place apart. The vodka came in handy. I had been in danger of becoming the thing I feared most. And this was it. I got a sitter quick and raced back through the years to North Beach. Grant Avenue was still there. But I was in for a shock. The Co-Existence Bagel Shop was gone gone gone. It's a video store now. My red-haired boy was gone as well, and I wondered idly where he might be at this moment, but then I looked at my watch and remembered the sitter and that was the end, the end forever of the red-haired boy. On the bus, I had this thought: There are two of us now who are no longer poets. It was freeing, in a way.

1972 After the unpaid labor of nursery school, kindergarten, the car pool, Head Start, Follow Through, and Parents in the Classrooms, it was by now the seventies. Holy shit, I thought: I've been a not-poet and a not-writer for over a decade now! When does the fun begin? My neighbor up the street was a professor at San Francisco State. I called him up and said, "I think there's still a faint trace of writer in me. I should probably go back to school." That's what everyone else seemed to be doing. Get in a program, get a life (although that particular phrase had not yet been invented). So my neighbor said: Go talk with Leonard Wolf (now known as The Father of Naomi Wolf—that's time warp for you). O.K. So I hired my twentieth babysitter—this one was Nadja—and raced over to San Francisco State to see what I had to do to be a writer. The babysitter was stoned when I returned, and both kids had contact highs, but I'm getting ahead of my tale. What a zoo. All these people milling about, and no one was in his or her office. It probably didn't help that I'd lost all sense of fashion during the childbearing years, and was, in fact, wearing an actual babushka on my head at the very door of Leonard Wolf's office. My neighbor friend was in the xerox room across the hall and he introduced me to Leonard Wolf. It was my lucky day. "Come on in," said Leonard Wolf as he unlocked his office, and in that moment the pile of manuscripts on his desk reached critical mass and everything fell swiftly to the floor. "What can I do for you?" he asked, unperturbed. This is what I said, in a voice pale from lack of use: "I want to be a writer." That was it. That was all.

I sat there in the sweater my son had recently thrown up on.

I sat there before Leonard Wolf in my fucking babushka. *And this is what he finally said:* "You want to be a writer? Go home and write. Did the great writers of the past go to graduate school? Did Emily Dickenson need an MFA from San Francisco State?" I saw I was in the presence of a true maverick. A person not unlike myself. What a relief! He was giving me permission to do the thing I most wanted to do—without theories, without analysis. Just as the writers of the past had done: trusting in memory, imagination, and desire. And the voices in their heads.

I went home and fed my family and picked up the toys. When all was quiet, I cleaned out the garage, put down a rug, got a lamp, and began to write. I wrote on an Olympia that my husband had given me before I knew I was a writer. I wrote hell out of that machine. It was a beauty. Every evening at eight, I'd read stories to the children. After nine, I kissed them goodnight and went into my garage and worked until the birds came up, or the sun, whichever got there first. I wrote my first novel, *Norma Jean the Termite Queen*, in five months flat. It was a labor of love and often, at 3 A.M., I would find myself doubled over laughing, I enjoyed writing that book so much. I still taught in the children's kindergarten and third grade classes. I offered them the same opportunity I'd given myself: to write their own poems and stories.

In the end, it all worked out. But it took more time than I thought it would. There was a war going on. Everyone I admired was getting shot to death. The kids grew. Some time around 1982, after the publication of my second novel, *Imaginary Crimes*, I began to think of myself as a writer. I could say that I began to forge an identity in those times: The Vietnam War, the new assumptions about women, about women writing, taking risks, writing as a profession. And it would be true. In retrospect, I know I had the writing in me all the time. *Thank you, Leonard Wolf, wherever you are. You saved me from graduate school and altered the course of my life.*

□

A Beginner

Bill Berkson

for Moses

A gypsy fortune teller once told my mother, "You will never be rich but you will always have beautiful things." By the time I came along, my parents had pretty well achieved their personal version of the American dream. They both earned good incomes by unflagging work at high-pressure jobs that suited them—my father as head of International News Service (he later became publisher of the New York *Journal-American*), and my mother as top publicist for American high fashion. The postwar years in our house were full of spirited Manhattan parties that mixed smart people from show business, journalism, and the fashion world. In some respects this "American Century" was still young, its insignias glittery arrivals in the foyer in dark topcoats and gentlemen's and ladies' hats, the women draped in fur wraps, coats and stoles. I shook hands politely in a navy blue suit, hair doused with my father's Bay Rum. In late adolescence I developed the habit of lecturing dinner guests on world events. Although my views on these matters were inclined in ways that would horrify most of this audience, I must have been fairly diplomatic in putting them across, because my mother would say afterward how impressed everyone had been by my good manners "and so mature."

Never having anticipated anything, I have always been astonished that anyone has a plan. After eighth-grade graduation, I walked across Central Park with my best friend Mason Hicks who told me that he knew exactly what he would do when he finished college—take over his uncle's nylon-stocking business in Knoxville, Tennesee. Not only did this strike me as exotic, but it was also incredible. Later another friend, Dick Nye, told me that he would succeed by going on to Harvard Business School and marrying a very rich man's daughter. Both did exactly as they predicted, and as far as I know it worked out well for them. For my part, between eleven and eighteen I knew only that the world of business was out and I wondered what else, if anything, there was for me. What place for all this energy in life? My fantasies ran to playing professional basketball (lucky to make the starting five at Trinity School) or crooning from a bandstand, a pop singer (I'm a monotone). The real-life alternatives, as I conceived them, were "beachcomber" and "soldier of fortune"—even so, the exact meaning of either term was lost on me. I was, as Paul Goodman would say, "growing up absurd."

It occurs to me now that, by limiting the number of books I read as a child, I intensified usefully what I retained of them. Except for newspapers, sports magazines, and comic books, including *Classics Comics,* which I continued to get well into high school, serious reading was for schoolwork only. How many book reports on *Kon-Tiki* can you write? Mainly I recall the poems assigned for memorizing: Milton's "On his Blindness," Shakespeare's "When in disgrace with fortune and men's eyes" and speeches from his plays. Frank Smith's Latin lessons stuck, and Paul Bolduc's French course helped prepare my ear for French poetry and Jean Gabin movies later. But scholastics generally were a blur. I was interested in sports and dancing and girls. Friday or Saturday night, often using the press passes my father had obtained, my friends and I went to the movies. Long afternoons were spent in my room listening alone to records. Everything else I studied by osmosis.

In my admissions interview at Lawrenceville I said, "Mathematics has always been my nemesis." Apparently that turn of phrase worked well enough, because I was admitted the following September. In Dawes House, the dormitory to which I was assigned, I fell in almost immediately with an elite group who made it their collective mission to get and read every book on the Modern Library backlist, the more dangerous the better ("dangerous" meant any sort of sex, spelled out or implied). We read most of Henry James, Radclyffe Hall, James T. Farrell's "Studs Lonigan" novels, Gide's *The Counterfeiters* and *The Immoralist,* what we could get of Lawrence and Henry Miller (*Chatterley* and almost all of Miller except *Air-Conditioned Nightmare* and his Big Sur book were banned, unavailable in America), *Point Counter Point, The Sun Also Rises* and Sartre's *Nausea.* Salinger's books were instant favorites—

not just *Catcher in the Rye* (which was of course about us, our preppie disaffections and furtive weekend adventures, and not the Christian allegory our teacher tried to twist it into) but also the stories of the Glass family, especially "A Perfect Day for Bananafish." Twenty years later, I set out to reread some of the books we read then and wondered what we found there, beyond the glamor of a fatalism that seemed equal to the raging uncertainties we were intent on playing out.

It was a dark and stormy night, I was sixteen and pitiful. I went down to the little office beside the front door of Dawes House and started writing. I had been composing somewhat lyrical diaries for about two years, and fictitious sports columns before that, but this had to be a poem: "What has love come to that . . ." I wrote twenty-two lines; some rhymed, others not, it looked plausible: "But for a single tender thought/I'd die someday." The next day I showed my poem, now typed on a fancy onion-skin sheet, to Mike Victor, who suggested taking it to Peter Fichter, the editor of *The Lit*. Fichter said, rather offhandedly it seemed to me, "I'd like to publish this in the next issue. Do you have any more?" "Yes," I said, reeling. That I may have become a poet because of a lie makes for some contrition. I knew nothing of the lives or characters of poets then. I had no particular taste. I went ahead, cutting classes, sitting and breaking rules by smoking in my dormitory room, obsessively typing poems in just about every format that seemed available at the time. I wrote one called "My Father's House" and another called "Threnody in Dust." One teacher, Frank Rouda, who had a good jazz collection and smoked mail-order Picayunes, gave me access to his library: I borrowed books by Henry Green, Gide's *Journals* and Gertrude Stein's *Three Lives*. I began writing stories. John Silver, with whose wife Cathy I worked later at *Art News*, read my poems carefully and lent me his copy of *Personae* by Ezra Pound, which was heavily annotated and from which I got the idea of poems as narration rather than responses to self-interviews, which the first ones had been. It must have been reading Pound that soon lead me to T. S. Eliot, whose poems were the source of most of my ideas—and education (I decided to read every work mentioned in the notes to *The Wasteland*, and then some)—for the next year. Beside Eliot, I imitated the "Camera Eye" sections of Dos Passos's *1919*. In the midst of this absorption I had a class with Thomas H. Johnson, the great Emily Dickinson scholar—gentle, informative, with no axe to grind, but glad to encourage me in my eagerness.

October of my senior year Russian tanks went into Hungary; James Michener came to lecture us about the frightful meaning of this act. My father said, "If you're going to be a writer, you need to know everything." I was in my last semester at Lawrenceville and in danger of failing chemistry. Instead, I got the mumps during final examinations week and stayed in the infirmary listening to the DJ William B. Williams play Fats Domino on the bedside radio. The chemistry teacher, Mr. Davis, (who had also coached me as a half-mile runner the previous spring) visited to say I would pass his course without having to take the exam. Then Mrs. Healy, the headmaster's wife, came and handed me a note transcribing something her husband, Allan, had said at Fifth Form Tea the day before: "That boy has his doubts, but he's going to be somebody." On graduation day I won awards for Best Long Essay and Best Poem (the prizes were Lloyd Frankenberg's *Pleasure Dome* and *The Collected Poems of e. e. cummings*). Under my picture in the yearbook, the *Olla Podrida* editors put a trumped-up motto, "Plato or comic books, I'm versatile." I was humiliated only insofar as at the time none of us could have known how apt a characterization they had made.

In 1957, I went from prep school to college and from tweeds and khakis to blue jeans and fatigues. That year everything moved ahead several paces with a synchronicity that still strikes me as impressive. At Brown, Gerald Weales glanced around the seminar table on the first day of his course on the Nature of Tragedy and said, "You may not know it, but you are all Existentialists." I knew because I had read *L'Étranger* by Camus in French class at Lawrenceville and Colin Wilson's *The Outsider* that summer while working at *Newsweek*. But I also knew the shock of finding that a poetry of moment was possible despite what had threatened to be an encirclement of dullness. "First came Patchen, then Ferlinghetti," as Ron Padgett says, and after them, *Howl*, *On the Road*, the first issues of *Evergreen Review* with Corso, Beckett, O'Hara—on up that ever-widening street.

A slightly older student from Detroit, Jim Davidson, expounded Keats's conception of the poet as "chameleon" with no separate entity of self. Jim introduced me to my first Greenwich Village bar, Julius's. He hoped to succeed in publishing or advertising. Hampered by a trick knee that worsened when he drank, he was found dead a year later on the tracks of the Lafayette St. IRT station. "Fell or was pushed," said the police report. I was called at dawn, together with another friend of his, to the morgue to identify the body.

Well-meaning and pernicious as stage mothers, most English teachers think it's just too great, if you are writing interestingly as a student, that you are writing at all. David Krause, an expert on Irish theater, was the first professor at Brown to encourage my writing. A review of Eliot's *On Poets and Poetry,* published in *Brunonia,* earned me permission to sit in on Hyatt Wagoner's graduate seminar on modern poets. S. Foster Damon was helpful in that, for his prosody course, he assigned simply the forms—the meter of Coleridge's *Cristobal*, dactylic hexameters, villanelles—to be filled by words in any order that fit, just to get the prescribed shape. John Hawkes gave me the first sense of professional conduct by saying one night after his short story workshop let out, "You and Steve Oberbeck are the writers. You should spend more time together." In class, Hawkes urged his charges, with a slightly demonic grin, to "write out of your childhood fears." He had little patience with my Kerouac imitations but liked my account of my friend Tony's strategy for eliminating raccoons from his Florida home.

Richard Foreman and the love of my freshman year, Joyce Ann Reed, were the stars of the theater group. (She was Antigone, he was Richard II and the father in *Desire Under the Elms*; Dick always played old men.) Likewise, Alvin Curran was already composing music (we wrote songs, words and music, for a silly musical about the Boston Tea Party, never completed). The next year, Richard Kostelanetz arrived, knowing everything about criticism. Clark Coolidge, also there (his father chaired the music department), was a close friend of Curran's, but Clark and I never actually met until the late sixties. The other poet was Ken Snyder—intense, pure, laconic, a Brando-type in style and looks, and interested, as I recall, in D. H. Lawrence. "Don't blame everything on America" was the corrective he offered when I showed him my diatribes in a series of poems called "Forty Dead Days." During Thanksgiving break in 1958, I visited San Francisco with my parents, ostensibly to secure a summer job on one of the newspapers, but really to search out the writers I thought would be there. North Beach was jammed with tour buses. I stood dumbfounded in The Place; asking if Gregory Corso or Allen Ginsberg might be around, I was given an unexpected clue, "All in New York, man!" The only poet I saw plain was pointed out to me after the bars closed: Jack Spicer, shoulders hunched, standing alone in the 2 A.M. fog on the traffic island at Broadway and Columbus.

On January 5, 1959, the day my father died, I left Providence and returned to live full-time in New York. That spring semester, while waiting to get accepted at Columbia for the fall, I decided to take classes at the New School for Social Research. Searching the catalogue, I saw that John Cage, whose name then rang some distant bell, was teaching Experimental Composition in a classroom at the school's 12th St. headquarters and, in the woods near his house in Stony Point, a course in mushroom identification. Pointless now to wonder if I didn't play it safe by signing up for, instead of one of Cage's offerings, William Troy's relatively standardized modern poetry course (for which I eventually wrote a paper trying to figure out Williams's "variable foot") and a poetry workshop taught by Kenneth Koch. Kenneth's class was held in the afternoon. Sitting very upright at one end of the long table, he invented as he went, uncertain in spots, but with surges of glee at the edges of his thought. Part of each lesson, the fun and suspense, was watching him wind toward describing graphically the pleasurable aspects of the poetry he liked—the poetry of Whitman, Rimbaud, Williams, Stevens, Auden, Lorca, Pasternak, Max Jacob, and Apollinaire, as well as of his friends Frank O'Hara and John Ashbery. Then, too, he would make an analogy between some moment in a poem and the sensibilities of New York painting—the amplitude of a de Kooning, Larry Rivers' zippy, prodigiously distracted wit, or Jane Freilicher's way of imagining with her paint how the vase of jonquils felt to be on the window sill in that day's light. All of these things would dovetail into the writing assignments Kenneth gave us, which were designed to (and really did) help precipitate and sustain energy and surprise in our poems. His attitude was such that whatever recognizable "talent" one brought into his class was strictly for openers, a responsibility to be taken care of, to enlarge.

Allen Ginsberg slid into a booth at the Cedar Bar to greet Paul Goodman, whom I had just met at a reading by Edward Dahlberg and Josephine Herbst at the Living Theater. (Still a junior beatnik, I had just given my first public poetry reading at the Seven Arts Coffee Gallery near 43rd St. on Ninth Ave., preceded by a young Haitian poet and Jack Micheline.) I was reduced to posturing while Paul next to me and Allen across the table traded remarks—a razzle-dazzle master class for this cute kid's benefit—on the poems of John Milton.

Try it this way: I come from a level of the upper urban middle class which, for generations, bred extraordinary dimness and repression. A level from which, to live, one must go down, or up, or out. I was not good at down. Up meant aristocratic pretensions or dandyism. Out meant crazy, drugs, fast cars or maybe art. I remember thinking that maybe some form of artistic dandyism was possible; it went (in the early sixties) with custom-made English suits, elegant women, and the kind of artistic persona I was constructing in my (like they say, "playful") poems. But to be a good dandy, one must lose circumspection (that side of so-called "common sense") and watch only the self made from the outside-in. There's no gainsaying advantage. The one time I met W. H. Auden, in 1967, he said, "It took me fifty years to understand that I belong to the same class as my parents." □

INFERNOS TO BATTLE

Jon Billman

I put in two aimless years in college at Iowa Wesleyan as, of all things, a physical education major, because I was determined only *not* to enter the adult world. Then a relationship dissolved, and I realized I needed a new direction. I sold my aluminum canoe for $75, bought a bus ticket, and went on the Trailways to Rapid City, South Dakota. I arrived in the middle of the night, walked around humping an army duffel bag until daylight, then hitchhiked to Lead in the northern Black Hills. There I began what I thought of as my career as a wildland firefighter.

The northern woods that summer were damp and cool and quiet. Every afternoon we would watch a cold thunderstorm roll over the Black Hills, bellyfull of hail. After work I'd saddle-up on my bicycle—mountain biking was still new and bikes were stiff and heavy and bombproof—and roll to Deadwood to meet the Nemo crew for a twenty-mile pedal through the hills followed by nickel beers and free popcorn at the Anaconda Casino.

That summer, two kids in Arizona dunked a lizard in gasoline, lit it on fire, set it down, and watched it scramble into the brush. Several days later we were sitting in the kitchen adjacent to the crew quarters, reading the sit. report off the wire: *Tonto Nat'l Forest, Historic Zane Grey Cabin Threatened.*

A lot of Zane Greys sat on a shelf under a mounted rattlesnake hide in the crew quarters. I had tried to read him, but could never finish one of his sagas. I got bored with his endless landscape details and with his characters, who, as far as I was concerned, were far less interesting than the firefighters I worked with, to say nothing of the Hell's Angels who bounced the bars in Deadwood and Sturgis. I had infernos to battle and a Nemo-district redhead to

17

chase on my bike. And I had Kentucky Fried Chicken! Original Recipe, delivered in the wilderness—dropped from the sky by a helicopter.

I had long been wary of the term "writer." Less so, perhaps, than "poet" or "novelist." With "writer," at least, comes the possibility that you earn your board with words. I admire journalists like Pete Hamill and Carl Hiassen, who wield word processors like flamethrowers during the day, work on the Great American Novel by lamplight, and throw in liberal doses of sportfishing. I admire writers like Tim Cahill, who set out to become a great novelist and, without apology, found himself paying the bills with great travel writing. A writer, by my narrow terms, must first be a *doer*. Zane Grey was a doer. I respect the hell out of the man—he gave up a dentistry career in New York— for his sportfishing records. He wrote hard and fished hard and lived a life worthy of writing about, wanting and getting more than a life of looking into people's mouths.

I thought I could hide behind the title "firefighter." The barmaid at the Buffalo Bar in Deadwood set me up with free draws when I introduced myself as a firefighter. Tourists used to buy us rounds in Dirty Nellies, a thanks for not letting a fire ruin their vacation.

I was sent to a fire in the Utah desert that had already burned out. The crew boss put us to work anyway, walking around kicking squirrel caches and smoldering stumps. I would wander away to hide under juniper trees, eat the extra Colorado peaches that I'd pinched from camp and stuffed into my firepack, and scratch notes that I thought of at the time as poetry. I had by then abandoned Zane Grey and discovered Thomas McGuane (a champion cutting-horse competitor and world-class fly fisherman, a doer) and Gary Snyder—I carried an old *Turtle Island* in my pack.

Mop-ups gave me long, dry hours to contemplate my future. I knew I wanted to play for a living. Someday, sure, I wanted to make a difference. As a firefighter, I knew I was only playing. The truth is, fire suppression American-style is counterproductive and a colossal waste of tax dollars. Besides, the only full-time Forest Service jobs available were being filled with women and minorities, or, ideally, minority women. Hell, I liked to read didn't I, maybe I could do something where I got to read. I declared my major back at school, English Education. I would become a teacher.

My mom still teaches home-ec—from her I learned to cook; I'm threatening to go to culinary arts school some day and learn enough about being a chef to be just a little dangerous. My dad taught art in public schools for thirty-nine years. I wished he had taken his own painting more seriously, but I suppose he made the adjustments he had to make. Now, in retirement, he's content to build bird houses and tie first-rate trout and salmon flies. Every couple of weeks I receive a manila envelope full of wooly buggers, hare's ears, nymphs. and renegades. But, I wish he'd pick up a paint brush again. In any case, he's always been a raconteur, like my grandfather, and some of my earliest memories are of listening to their stories. My idea of my dad at work is of him playing with paint and clay all day and getting paid for it; of course, that had very little to do with the realities of teaching, but I wanted to get paid for something like that.

I took my best offer from Kemmerer, Wyoming, which turns out to be a kind of end of the road. Teachers move here because they were fired somewhere else or are hiding from something or someone. Some people teach here after teaching on the reservation, a small step up for them. My first day of school, before the first bell, I had to step in between two seventeen-year-old cowboys fighting outside my room—I'm six-feet-one and I looked up at both of them. While supervising Tuesday-night detention, I sat on a tack one of the delinquents put on my chair, requiring me to get a tetanus booster. A Mormon parent went to the school board to have me fired because a student in her daughter's class read aloud a poem with "fucking" used as an adjective. Most new teachers stay here one year. I lasted two.

Toward the end of my brief term in the ninth grade, I would write while my students took tests. Write during films. Write during teachers' meetings. I appeared to be taking diligent notes. I wrote of the world around me, the characters I worked with, the charlatans I worked for, the few females in town, a wild red-headed mining engineer, frontier ministers, bad Mormons and good Mormons. I turned my scribbles into a story that was, I now see, abominable, but it got me into graduate school! So writing is what saved me from becoming an alcoholic or worse.

Eastern Washington University must have needed my money, because I got in with out-of-state graduate tuition and no breaks other than the hair shirt that is my student loan.

I invited myself to my favorite teacher's farm for Thanksgiving dinner. Hell, I thought, I've sacrificed to get here, I'm gonna absorb everything in two years, gonna see the elephant. John Keeble had also invited Dan Sisson, who writes for *Field and Stream*. We ran bird dogs and I asked them questions all day and didn't leave until after dark. That afternoon John gave me the best writing advice I've ever heard. He said, simply, "Write hard."

Then Howard Junker, the editor of *ZYZZYVA*, liked one of my stories. He worked on it with me for almost a year, and I learned as much from that process as I did in my two years of M.F.A.

After graduation, I went back to the woods.

It took about a month before I realized I'd outgrown firefighting. I'd read an article about how a day on the fireline is like smoking five cartons of cigarettes. I didn't have health insurance and I needed to do something less solipsistic, something that mattered more. So I left the Black Hills with the idea of writing for a living. I moved my pickup-load of possessions into a cabin in northern Utah. I was prepared to winter and write and fulfill another desire that had been with me much longer than my desire to write: to be a ski bum. I bought a new chainsaw, a season pass to Beaver Mountain, and a new pair of Karhu telemark skis.

In the fall, writing time was spent cutting and hauling the pine, spruce, and aspen that would get us, my wife-to-be and I, through the winter. Once winter hit, I spent most of my writing time skiing. Groceries (with heavy racks of bottled beer and bags of bulk garlic) had to be pulled uphill in a *pulk* made out of an ordinary children's sled. Dirty laundry had to be skied down, driven to town; clean laundry pulled back up. I skied manuscripts to the post office, rejection letters back up to use as fire starter. At night, for entertainment—no TV—we cooked elaborate meals of elk and trout, drank good beer and jug wine, made love, and listened to radio stations from as far away as Los Angeles and Calgary. I read Stephen Ambrose and Faulkner, Charles Darwin, Robert Stone, and the Bible. Spring—mud season—was spent doing carpentry work on the old cabin.

I grew strong that year; mere living required physical work. I grew stronger mentally as well, strong in my sense of what writing should be. I finished my manuscript, ran out of money, and took a one-year job in town, back in Kemmerer, this time teaching seventh grade. I didn't have an agent, few contacts, only the determination that this would be my last teaching job. I sent my book manuscript out like grapeshot, no allegiances, no loyalties; as long as someone still had my manuscript and hadn't rejected me, I had hope. As an afterthought, I mailed a copy to the zip code of Annie Proulx, who had recently moved to Wyoming to fish, ski, canoe, and hide. Two days later she called me. "Who *are* you?" she asked. Then she sent my manuscript to her own agent: my lucky break. My first book, a collection of fiction, *When We Were Wolves*, was published by Random House in the summer of '99.

I'm still self-conscious about calling myself a writer. This is dangerous, because I get asked to speak at Rotary and back at the high school. The students in my college-outreach night class like the idea that their instructor is a writer, but it's funny that not one of them has ever asked to see my work.

My new work clothes are flannel pajamas. I don't wear a wristwatch. I turn west at the coffee machine, and half a minute later I'm seated at my desk, a Korean-era army-clerk's desk that Ron, a wildlife biologist who wants to be a writer, helped me move—it was made from the melted-down carcass of a jeep, he says. In any case, my best ideas come when I'm skiing or running.

I realize my collection of stories was just my foot in the door; I'm under a daunting contract to write a novel, which is what I'm doing now, head down, not looking up for fear of seeing the beast that is the possibility of writing seven hundred pages of horseshit and not knowing it until I've finished. Worse yet is taking mincing little steps through the process and not writing the hell out of what you know, but what a small part of you thinks someone else wants to hear.

An old lady cornered me in the local museum recently, suspicious of me because it was daytime and I wasn't at the mine, a real job. She said, "I hear you're getting a book published." Yes, I told her, I am. She narrowed her eyes. Her nose wrinkled back. Through bright pursed lipstick she said, "*That* must be costing you a bundle." □

WHAT I HID
& WHAT WAS FOUND

Justin Chin

*A*sk any good Chinese family. The pecking order of desirable professions are: Doctor (neurosurgeon or cardiac surgeon is best; and, failing a career in medicine, dentistry is an acceptable runner-up). Lawyer. Engineer. More liberal families would probably accept Accountancy, and possibly an M.B.A. from an American Ivy League university. If you were artistic, you might be an architect.

These professions conferred upon the practitioner's parents bragging rights of the highest order, and these rights were used to great effect in smiting down kith and kin. A well-timed brag on the battle grounds of golf courses and Aquarobics could transform others into bitter green-eyed monsters and elevate one's standing in society.

Writing was just not done. Sure, it was *done*, but by the children of poor sad parents who had to sit tight-lipped at family dinners and (horrors!) class reunions, where they had to endure scads of pity and scorn. If any writing was ever done, it was done For Fun and, possibly, to win essay contests so that, again, the parents could rub it into the faces of relatives who had lesser children.

This was Singapore in the eighties. Enough time had passed since the country had gained its independence, first from British colonial rule, then from the Japanese Occupation, and then from the collective peninsula of Malaya. This was the time when children born of parents from those riotous days of the race-conscious sixties were making their mark on The Great Society. Their parents had given them an independent country-state, and now it was time for the children to make good on those droning when-we-were-your-age lectures their parents had launched into at every opportunity.

Education was the equalizing factor among races and social classes. Do well in subjects that mattered, which were the sciences and the maths, and, boyo, you were in. Everybody admired you. People saw in you hope, redemption, and Great Things. The kids brought up in this atmosphere were very much co-conspirators. Visions of mansions in the twisty roads of chichi Commonwealth Avenue or bungalows in the Bukit Timah hills danced in their eyes.

At home, we had tuition for as many subjects as were deemed needed. After school, some poor hapless graduate who could not get a real job would come to our house and give us extra lessons in math, Chinese, and the sciences. Our parents bought assessment books that textbooks companies churned out by the ton. These were workbooks chock-full of difficult math sums, baffling chemistry and physics problems, with the correct answers in the back of the book. Many of these very same questions had once appeared in state examinations. Rumour had it that they might appear again in any given year. So parents, teachers, and children all furiously worked them into the fabric of their lives.

There were English assessment books, too, full of grammar exercises, designed to help one learn tenses, vocabulary, sentence construction, punctuation, and all those idiomatic things to do with the English language. There were also English composition books, with exemplary essays, all written in crisp, perfectly constructed English sentences. No run-ons, no postmodern meanderings, just perfect little clause/phrase or phrase/clause sentences, with one exclamation point thrown in somewhere to give a spark of life. Some of my classmates at school memorized a whole bank of these compositions so that they could regurgitate them at exam time, scribbling them down from memory word for word.

We were also given sample answers for our English literature classes, so we could give correct answers to Shakespeare, Achebe, and *The Crucible*. In Secondary One (seventh grade), the penultimate year of our general education, where we still had art class, a classmate of mine even enrolled in art tuition, where his art tutor made him practice the same two drawings all semester so that he would ace that final art exam.

The act of writing was seen as something wholly self-indulgent, as a complete waste of time. In a country where the press, the theater, the cinema, were closely monitored by the government, writing was also an act that could conceivably get someone into real trouble. Writing seemed, like a dangerous temptation—to actually speak one's mind might be to say something against the grain, to challenge authority.

Our parents had lived through the creation of the Internal Security Act. They had witnessed communists, communist sympathizers, opposition party leaders, and people who were vocally critical of the government arrested and detained without trial. Their reputations were ruined by scandolous stories in the government-controlled newspapers. "Better not say anything, better not make waves," we were warned. "Much better you go study and become a doctor. Make loads of money. After all, in the end, it's money that talks." Writing did not promise wealth of any sort.

There were local writers and local playwrights, but they were looked on as *the artistic crowd*: effeminate poofters, bored housewives, and people with real jobs who wrote as a hobby. These were people who entertained with their talent, but did not contribute in any great way to The Scheme of Great Things.

Occasionally, there would be a blip on the screen. A play would be closed down, a book banned.

Once, a playwright was commended for his play about the plight of Filipino maids in Singapore. Two years later, however, the government found out that the playwright was friendly with people who may have had communist leanings. And his play was denounced, held up as an example of subversive communist propaganda.

Recently, members of a local theater company were hauled in for questioning—and their company's rights to perform yanked—after it was discovered that some members of the group had attended Augusta Boal's Theatre of The Oppressed Workshop in New York City. How did the government *know*, some wondered (but did not ask publicly). In the end, everyone knew that the government just knew things.

Most of the time, writers simply accepted such repression. They grumbled, they griped, and they dreamed of the freedoms of the West.

I enjoyed reading more than anything else. By the time I was in Primary Three, I was reading at a level higher than my grade, starting with Enid Blyton books, and then Agatha Christie mysteries. I enjoyed these fantasy worlds, these other realities, these *stories*.

Inspired by our reading, a friend and I excitedly tried our

hand at writing our own little stories. Somehow, the other kids in the class managed to create these fabulous stories that were printed in the school annual. Now, twenty years later, I suspect that their parents may have helped them, but then, even as I was proud of my piddly little achievement, it crushed me to realize that my nine-year-old mind could not keep up with all these other minds around me. Worse than that, my mother found a story that I had written, tucked away in my school bag. It was a twee plotless illustrated-with-colored-pencils thing: some space guy gets captured by aliens, he blasts them with a laser gun, and escapes. But I had had trouble with "than" and "then," and my mom was livid. Besides wasting my time on such a worthless non-academic activity, how could I also not know such a simple thing? I was severely scolded and that evening's television-viewing privileges rescinded. I was made to write twenty sentences using "then" and twenty using "than" correctly. My first stab at writing a story ended up in tears.

It was *then* that I hid my fondness for writing in my English composition classes rather *than* be berated and put down for my hobby. (Yes, like stamp-collecting and comic books, that was the only thing it was allowed to be. My parents tried to persuade me to switch hobbies to chess, a much better hobby since it used the brain.)

I tore into my assignments like mad, writing essays and narratives. All through my school years, while my classmates hated to write these compositions once a week, I was secretly delighted. It was the only thing I was good at. I had been sent to the science sequence and I was not doing well. I had above-average grades, but that wasn't going to be good enough to get me into medical school, was it? Nothing but straight A's were expected.

My father was one of the first in his side of the family to go to university, medical school, and on scholarship, no less. It was no small feat. My grandad, the jolly old bigamist, was a butcher (we always had the best cuts of pork). He had twelve children and two wives to support, so money was tight. Accomplishment and success were important things to the family. Dad met Mom when he was a resident working off his scholarship obligations. She was the night nurse on the ward. (I'm glad I wasn't a patient on that ward on that night, presumably not much hospitaling was done while the night nurse and the night doctor were making goo-goo eyes at each other and plotting to go to the Rose Show on the weekend.)

Mom had come to that profession by defying her own father, who balked at his daughter becoming a nurse. Good girls from good families became teachers, not nurses, swabbing at syphilitic sores and changing geriatrics' bedpans.

When your parents are both in the medical profession, everyone and the cat simply assumes that the children would be doctors, too. Sitting in the back of my dad's clinic, patients often asked when my brother and I were going to take over our dad's practice, and this was when we were still in primary school. The notion of taking over the family business is a very Chinese thing. And when the family business was something as prestigious as medicine, the stakes were raised.

Among my school chums, the ones whose fathers or mothers were doctors all knew they were to follow suit. One school chum's father even pulled every string, calling in favors from friends on the board of directors and the chair of Old Boys' Association, so that his daughter, who had never even taken a science class in her school life, could rectify her shameful mistake and be enrolled in the science sequence. She flunked horribly.

In an effort to make me study more, I was forbidden to read any books that were not curriculum-related. Anytime I was caught reading a non-textbook, I was scolded. For a few years, I even gave up reading altogether.

Then one day a few years later, I discovered an old book of my late uncle's. It was the collected works of Oscar Wilde. This fat tome with its funny/sad fairy tales, and weird and beautiful stories, rekindled my love for reading. I started borrowing books from the school library and the British Council library. I wandered in bookstores looking at books I could not afford to buy, taking note of their names so I could find them in the libraries.

I hid my reading, too: I read on the schoolbus and after everyone had gone to bed. Occasionally, my grandmother, shuffling to the toilet late at night, would stick her head into my room and catch me lying in bed with a book. She would nag me for not studying and threaten to tell my parents.

Reading also refueled my wanting to write. So, once a week, I looked at the assignment on the blackboard and delved into writing. It could have been an argumentative essay, or those assignments requiring the student to finish a narrative given the first few lines. I wrote feverishly and happily, my pen pressed into the ruled notebook, until my fingers were cramped. It was a feeling I loved, how those digits ached and how the muscles hurt as I pulled my fingers back to crack my knuckles in order to relieve the pressure. My grades for my compositions were nothing exceptional, but, in the dreary hours of school, it was the most enjoyment I got.

I did not think that I wanted to be a writer. I wanted to be an actor. I had acted in a school production, a multicultural production of *The Diary of Anne Frank,* where the Franks and the Van Daams were Chinese, Muslim, and Indian, and I was hooked. I had done this without my parents' knowledge, and by the time they found out, it was too late to yank me out of it. The play did well and was one of three plays selected to be part of that year's Arts Festival Fringe.

I wanted a life in the theater. Already, my mom had cautioned me about people in the theater. She warned me that a lot of them were "funny."

"You mean like comedic?" I replied innocently.

"No . . . homosexual!" she whispered, hesitatingly. If she only knew: I had been having sex with men ever since I was thirteen. Maybe all little queers find their way to the drama club one way or another.

I started hanging around the local theater scene. It was the first time I had socialized with other gays. I had avoided the queens at school, because I did not want any of the teasing and bullying they endured to be redirected toward me. Hanging out with the out-and-out gays in the theater helped me overcome my own homophobic hangups. I started being comfortable even around the screamingest queens.

In the theater world, it seemed, writers were revered, and I wanted that kind of adoration. I also wanted the power that writers in the theater seemed to wield. Again, inspired by all my reading and from watching stage productions, I thought that I, too, could write something fabulous, perhaps a truly subversive account of gay life in Singapore in the late eighties. I would be the toast of the scene, profiled in the arts section of the *Straits Times,* where Dinesh D'Souza, the lispy theater critic and rumored porno-maven who preferred little Noorlinah Muhammad's over-enunciated performance as Anne in *The Diary of Anne Frank* to my stately, multifaceted, brooding Peter, would be amazed by my brilliance.

Wouldn't that show my folks what was what.

I withdrew money from my savings account, dashed down to Yaohan Electronics, and bought a typewriter (which I still have). I took my first babysteps at writing. I was a Day-Glo existentialist (hey, it was the eighties), writing purple prose and utterly overblown pretentious poetry about death, ennui, and the ickiness of Life ("The seed of Eve spat from my mouth/lies barren in the futile soil!") Fueled by pop music, I descended further into the ungodly realm of Hallmark schmaltz. I was headed for the saccharine swamplands ruled by Susan Poliz Schultz.

After royally fucking up my examinations, I came to the United States to take another stab at an education. Here, I quickly learned that I was a bad actor. More horrifyingly, I was a bad ethnic actor. I had this strange accent, I was completely untrained, and I was completely uncomfortable in my body. I realized that I had never been any good and that my landing a role in a school production had less to do with talent than with the limited number of boys in the drama club who weren't queens who wanted to wear wigs and dresses and pile on Max Factor. I also knew that I would not get better, no matter how I tried. Besides, I could not bring myself to take acting classes. Yikes, that would be frivolous! self-indulgent! a waste of time! wrong! My socialization had run deep grooves into me.

In my first semester at an American college, I felt I had to pick a major and so I chose journalism. It seemed like a practical choice and it combined the best of both worlds—what I enjoyed doing and the prospects of getting a Real Job.

At Hawaii Pacific College, where they accepted anyone with a pulse, I enrolled in first-year English. One of the assignments was to do some creative work. The lecturer held up my work to the class as an example of "powerful" and "emotional" writing. In actuality, it was just plain bad; it was the poetic equivalent of the power ballad—all syrup, manipulation, and easy payback. Ms. Fischel enjoyed the Chippendales, Michael Bolton, and Kenny G; I should have known better. But I was pleased and held my head up high.

After that semester, I transferred to the University of Hawaii. In my first semester there, I sorted through the schedule and signed up for a writing class that fit my schedule. By some sheer stroke of luck, I ended up meeting the writer formerly known as Faye Kicknosway. (She has since changed her name to Morgan Blair.) She was a tough broad, weird in a mid-Western writerly way, and quite intense. Sitting in her cramped sunny little office by a bookshelf towering with little chapbooks, she scribbled comments on my poems. No, she said, this doesn't work, and this, and this. Fix it! she exhorted. My heart felt like it had been poked with big sharp sticks. I wanted to cry. She was brutal. I pulled out the big guns, those poems from the previous semester that Ms. Fischel had loved. Faye glanced at them, looked me straight in the eye, and said, No, don't ever do that ever again. She was the first person to take my writing seriously enough not to humor me.

It was enough to make anyone want to throw in the penwipes. One day, I turned in two pieces, and, to my surprise, she loved them. She offered suggestions on how to shape them. Her upper-level class was going to do a reading, and she invited me to read with them.

When I showed up at the dry-run of the reading, I was nervous and intimidated. But it was also to be the turning point of my life, the start of my life as a writer. At the rehearsal, there were two writers who wowed me. One was a sassy local woman who wrote poems in the voice of a *tita*, and the other was this well-groomed fey Filipino guy with big sculpted hair who wrote hilarious poems about his mother and about cruising the men's bathrooms at Sinclair Library. During the break, the two of them came up to me arm in arm and said how much they loved my work. They were Lois-Ann Yamanaka and R. Zamora Linmark. We talked and Lois-Ann invited me to join a writing workshop they had.

Soon, every Sunday afternoon, Lisa Asagi, another of Faye's students, and Zack would pick me up and we would drive to Kalihi to Lois-Ann's house. We'd whip out our poems and read our work to each other and then proceed to workshop them. We'd recommend books to each other, buy books for each other, and lend each other books. We stalked Jessica Hagedorn when she came to Hawaii. Armed with *The International Directory of Little Magazines and Small Presses*, and ragged copies of *Poets & Writers*, we encouraged each other to send our work out to various journals and presses. We comforted and kvetched when we were rejected, rejoiced and feigned jealousy when someone was published. We all wrote very differently, but we understood each other's voice and processes and aesthetics.

Lisa, Zack, and I used to hang out a lot on the weekends, drinking heavily (Lisa conveniently worked at the Liquor Collection at Ward Warehouse) and going clubbing. Lying on the floor in Zack's Waikiki apartment, we wrote poems and stories chronicling our obsessive love interests, our screwed-up romantic and familial relationships, our mad wild lives. We were queer for Anaïs Nin (but we now know better—that she was just a slut with a diary), Lorca, García Márquez, Barthes, Genet, Winterson, Jane Bowles. We shared our writing with each other at every opportunity. We inspired and goaded each other to create new work. We supported each other unequivocally, and we developed a language of our own that allowed us to turn the stuff of our queer little lives into something real on the page.

With Lisa, Zack, Lois-Ann, and Faye, we never second-guessed that we were anything but writers. It was that tits-to-the-wind abandon that gave me permission to believe that it was O.K. to be a writer, and that I was one.

I visited San Francisco in the summer of 1990. I went to as many readings as I could. I saw Diane DiPrima, Sharon Olds, Galway Kinnell, Robert Hass, Allen Ginsberg, Judy Grahn, and a bunch of obscure poets at Small Press Traffic whose names I have forgotten. Every Thursday night, I went to Café Babar for the open readings. The corrugated tin walls and the second-hand smoky air reverberated with an intensity that was exhilarating. Poets were heckled with unrestrained candor and applauded with genuine admiration and respect. Of course, in all the weeks that I went there, I never had the nerve to read my own work. I returned to Hawaii in the fall, filled with what I had witnessed in San Francisco—the street poetry and all its verve, the people who flocked to literary readings, the used bookstores full of treasures, Small Press Traffic's shelves brimming over with these little books, each one painstakingly put together by someone not unlike myself—a world of possibilities that, until then, I never knew existed. I knew I had to move to San Francisco.

Since then, R. Zamora Linmark has published *Rolling the R's*, a highly acclaimed debut novel, and is currently in Manila on a Fulbright finishing his new novel. Lois-Ann Yamanaka has published three books to a certain amount of acclaim and controversy and was recently featured on the cover of *Poets & Writers*. Lisa Asagi has published stories in various journals, and we are all looking forward to her first novel, if she ever gets her shit together to finish it. Borders has opened a twenty-four-hour store (in the middle of Singapore's tourist district) which is so busy the clerks can only restock from midnight to 6 A.M.

Occasionally, my mom calls and cautions me to not write anything bad about the government (or anything at all about the family).

Recently, the Malaysian police arrested two people for what they had written in their e-mails. In the throes of the country's failing economy, the two had *dared* suggest that there was a smidgen of racial tension in the land. They were charged with "gossip mongering" and were detained without trial for two years in order to "preserve national security."

In my life, writing has been and still is something that is dangerous, politically and privately. The act of writing occupies a limboland. It is necessary but feared.

Even writing this piece fills me with a certain dread. It is a risk that I take on, because I know no better way to make sense of this mud of life. Everyday I have to fight my feelings that what I do is not trivial, not frivolous, not meaningless. In the end, in the dustbin of my personal history, whether my work survives is not the issue. What I know is that it was done: It gave me the courage to speak and to find some semblance of myself. And that small act has loosened the straps on that old muzzle made in the government store and sent to every home. □

DUBIOUS QUEST

Blair Fuller

I read with painful slowness. I opened the children's books pressed on me with a kind of dread, and reached the tenth or twentieth page of very few. My handwriting was so illegible that teachers despaired of making it out.

That was my literary situation in the sixth grade. To remedy it my homeroom teacher attempted to teach me to write left-handed. I was kept in the classroom during many bitter recesses learning to make letters with my left hand, but my left-handed script turned out to be at least as botched as my right.

I was sent to boarding school starting with my eighth-grade year. The Fountain Valley School was two-and-one-half days by train from New York, a world away from home, but although frightened at first, I did not regret this.

My mother had recently divorced and remarried. I liked my stepfather, and my new stepbrothers even more—I had known them all my life. At the same time, however, I had Hamletish resentments that my stepfather had usurped my father's place. My father had been the architect of the house in which I and my two sisters had grown up, and I felt his banishment from it as an injustice.

"Your mother had the money to build the house, she owns it," my father told me, but I thought of it as one of "his houses," a house that he "had done," phrases I'd often heard referring to houses that he had designed.

Art, which certainly included design, had been given paramount importance in family conversations. As I had understood it, Michaelangelo's *David* was Michaelangelo's. It was not the city of Florence's or whoever-had-paid-for-it's *David*.

Another fact complicated my thoughts and feelings: My

mother had sculpted two-thirds life-size, bas relief, cast terra-cotta plaques of Adam and Eve which were set into niches on the back side of the house facing the garden. My father had been the model for "most" of her Adam. He would have been perfect, she used to declare, except that he "needed an inch or two more between the knee and the ankle." She had added the inch or two without affecting Adam's and my father's resemblance. I would sometimes go out in back to look at him, fig-leafed, with his head in profile looking heavenward. The man made in God's image.

My father's martini-time announcement to me of the divorce shocked and upset me, but my mother's reasons for divorcing him were not a mystery—although they were never spoken about plainly. "Incompatibility" was spoken about, but without knowing the words for these things I knew my father was destructively alcoholic, intellectually arrogant, a seducer of other women, and in a state of self-pitying anger because his architectural practice and his own, much-celebrated early promise had dwindled through the Great Depression. Gone from the house, and suddenly much poorer, he hit out at stand-ins for the roots of his troubles—bankers and politicians, old friends and enemies, and even myself: "I think any boy born with money in this country has two strikes against him from the start."

During my weekend visits with him I was continually anxious about what missed connection or misunderstanding, what moments of altercation or embarassment in bars or restaurants, might occur, and this was very painful. I wanted to and managed still to admire him greatly. He had been a star athlete, an excellent student, an elected class officer at Harvard, and one of the first men to be commissioned a US Navy pilot. He had flown submarine patrols over the English Channel in 1917–18. These wonderful accomplishments seemed well beyond my own possibilities. But why was he acting as he was? Neither my older sister—who visited him separately—nor I, told our mother of the difficulites of those weekends. Our mother wanted only good news, and her questions were phrased so that it was probable she would receive it.

" . . . I'm sure you'd like that, wouldn't you?"

" . . . You had a good time, I hope?"

She—like my father's old friends when they would speak to me about him—spoke still of his extraordinary "charm" and "brilliance."

I puzzled over the meanings of those words. Better to be two thousand miles away than uneasy with one parent, distant from the other, and confused about the validity, the reality under the appearance, of the ideas and people most familiar to me.

First seen, and every time seen, the granite of Pike's Peak standing fourteen thousand feet high, twenty miles to the west of Fountain Valley looked undeniably real, bare and ungiving, figuratively insurmountable, and, at rare moments, inspirational. My reading and writing skills still were poor, but I had developed a twelve-year-old's version of a jock persona, and once I'd found the playing fields I felt that I would make my way.

My literary education began in an English class taught by Edward "Ned" Risley, someone just out of college who had the manners of an energetic and jocular wise guy. He assigned us to read John Steinbeck's *In Dubious Battle,* a novel of owner-labor conflict in California orchards, and after I had read it I, feeling very shy and unaccustomed, asked Risley if there were other books like Steinbeck's I could read.

He took an immediate, vivid interest, but muted it, made it a confidential matter between us out of consideration, I believe, for my timidity. "Hang on, Sport. We'll talk about this." With me, after that, he was never a wise guy.

He sent me to the school library, and I began to read with the benign help of the librarian, who was the wife of the chief teacher of science, a small woman, soft-voiced, with a pretty smile. Perhaps she and Risley had spoken about me. I soon often dreamt of her.

I read contemporaries, serious writers, not because I enjoyed reading in the usual sense. The process was still arduous. But because Steinbeck, Thomas Wolfe, James T. O'Farrell, Pearl Buck, and, later, Hemingway, and more, presented me with clear pictures of how lives that were not the lives of my parents were lived, lives that were not my own life, either—not yet, certainly —but were lives I might encounter and that my own might possibly come to resemble.

None of the books I absorbed offered "escape." To be sure, some stories swept me into their narratives, but if they lacked a ring of truth I would quickly abandon them. It was reality I was after and these books came to seem the most important of my studies.

After two years at Fountain Valley I was told that I would be transferring to Deerfield Academy. My father's family had owned and worked a farm a mile south of Deerfield since the early nineteenth century—one of his first cousins was currently running it—so that there was a supposed family-history reason for the change. My absences between Christmases and the summer vacations had been five months long and it was thought I would be happier closer to home. I doubted this, but could not say so out loud. That Risley was leaving Fountain Valley to enter training as a US Army pilot made it easier.

I was unhappy at Deerfield. One of my first questions to the teacher in charge of my dormitory was, "Where is the library?" Instead of giving me directions he questioned my motives. What was it I wanted to read? Having heard my response, he said that, perhaps, if my grades turned out to be good enough, perhaps later such reading would be permissible. My grades were mediocre, and I never found the library.

The concept of "image," as in a corporate "image," had not yet been invented, but Deerfield was dedicated to its own image in a single-minded way. Just down the highway the late President, Calvin Coolidge, had been Mayor of Northampton, and it was he who had declared that "The business of America is Business."

Deerfield's legendary headmaster, Frank Boyden, certainly believed so, and the school's objective was to prepare its students for the SAT exams which would gain them admittance to prestigious colleges, whence they would be expected to start up corporate ladders. We students were told parables of corporate success, and were required to wear jackets and neckties like white-collar nine-to-fivers. Our desks must be bare of books and papers not in current use, which was said to be the custom of top executives. Our walls must be hung with pictures suitable to conservative taste—properly framed and placed.

The corporate style extended to chain-of-command authority. There was no student government or class or domitory representation—not helpful to boys of our age, the headmaster explained, such imitations of adult self-government could only make possible the expression of disruptive ideas. National politics, "great ideas," were not discussed.

I found all this stifling. Eventually, wanting the feeling of freedom, I discovered how to get out of my dormitory undetected after lights out. I would furtively cross the highway and the train tracks to smoke illicit cigarettes in a cemetery where some of my forebears were buried.

One warm night in spring I went in the opposite direction, across Main Street, and skulked through backyards and down to the playing fields. By the Deerfield River, which I knew to be nicely concealed by the suddenly green-leafed trees, I found a dozen boys like myself, smoking and even drinking beer, or simply sitting and talking.

I was overjoyed. They and I were being ourselves, at least, acting on our own, speaking whatever thoughts we had, while what Deerfied was requiring of us was charade. The bombing of Pearl Harbor and our entry into World War II the past December had not changed by an iota the school's preoccupations and demeanor. When I crossed paths on campus with one of the river-boys during the day, we did not acknowledge our acquaintance.

My older stepbrother, sympathizing with my unhappiness, helped persuade my mother that I should return to Fountain Valley rather than continue at Deerfield. I was grateful to him. By then it had become difficult for me to talk to any and all adults. I felt this as a deficit and knew that it was irritating to my parents and others, but my tongue would grow thick, too clumsy for speech.

Back at Fountain Valley I learned immediately that Ned Risley had been killed flying an Army Air Force P-38 on a training flight. His plane had crashed on the prairie east of, and not very far from, Fountain Valley. The day of the crash was said to have been cloudless and without any apparently difficult conditions.

Risley had been in love with the headmaster's daughter—we students had all observed his infatuation with sly ribaldry or sympathy, or both. Now I was told that she had rejected his proposal of marriage. Had he, in fact, committed suicide by crashing the plane? This was very quietly talked about.

I thought of attempting to find the crash scene, but that was impractical. What I imagined it to have been, a hard-baked sandy landscape punctured by prairie-dog holes, with tumbleweeds bouncing gently through on the endless winds, became sharply etched in my mind.

That winter I wrote an assigned story for English class. When it came back, it bore the usual, large portion of corrections and critical comments, but also the grade of B-minus. I believe that it was the first B, even though a minus, that I had ever received in English.

To my astonishment the English teacher, Alex Campbell, then asked if he could print the story in the school literary magazine. But he said that if I wanted him to do so, I would have to change the ending, which seemed too extreme.

In the story a boy much like myself leaves his house on a clear, still night and climbs a neighboring hill. He sits and thinks of the many lives being lived in the houses whose lights he can see, not only of their number but of the complexities of their relationships, their ambitions and troubles, and then of the vast number of humans and other creatures and situations in the world beyond his vision. He craves knowledge of all that he does not know, of all that will be forever beyond his experience and grasp.

As I had written the story, it ended with the boy, feeling defeated by his limitations before such vastness, taking his own life. Campbell said that that seemed too unlikely, the boy should just get up and go home, which would be a likely enough ending. Alive and well, I had to agree.

When the story was printed, it was read at home. I do not remember what exactly was said about it, but I felt that I had done something that altered the ideas people had of me. My stepfather said something like, "very interesting," a phrase which was about as far as he would go in enthusiasm. He was a publisher and he became a very well-known one in the course of his long career, Cass Canfield of Harpers.

I was pleased, but I had known Cass long enough to know that what excited him in books only rarely excited me, and vice versa. Cass was most interested in books he had imagined and found someone to write, chief among them John Gunther's *Inside* books, which began with *Inside Europe* and eventually covered the continents. Secondly, he was fascinated by histories; he courted many public figures for their memoirs. Only thirdly did he appreciate novels, usually the Harper books that sold very well like Louis Bromfield's and Betty Smith's *A Tree Grows in Brooklyn*.

Cass had spent a few years in England when he had first become a publisher, and he published several distinguished English authors, particularly J. B. Priestley and Aldous Huxley, and he respected them and cherished their acquaintance, but he did not find Americans of their power.

I never thought of my own enthusiasms as being opposed to Cass's, only that they were different, and thinking about the differences helped me both to see my own way and to understand the difficulties of commercial publishing.

Meager beginnings, these seem to me, now that I have written them down, yet lacking in confidence though I was, lacking clear or practical objectives, I was on a track.

As an enlisted man, then a petty officer, serving on a destroyer escort converted to a small personnel transport ship, I tried in my spare time to teach myself to type on the radio shack's machines, while making notes on the terrifying destruction by Japanese and American bombardment of Manila, and the chaos there in which American soldiers and sailors—the winners—were indulging every sexual and acquisitive whim and treating the Phillipinos as "gooks."

Discharged and working in New York while I waited to go to college, I went at night to a secretarial school to improve my typing.

The summer following my freshman year at Harvard (which admitted me partially, at least, because I was a "legacy"), I and a friend worked as roustabouts with the sideshow of the King Brothers Three Ring Circus, working next to the hooves of Susie, the elephant, to haul up the tent, and hammering in the stakes that would hold the guylines with twelve-pound sledges. We quit when the circus headed south from New England, and I attempted to write an article about the experience, a first, clumsy and unsuccessful, but inspiring try.

Back in college I took a writing course from a true professional, Kenneth Payson Kempton, a man who wrote children's books, *Saturday Evening Post* stories—if someone wanted it he could write it—and took me seriously. And the *Harvard Advocate* published a short story of mine.

I worked one long summer as a United Press correspondent in the Detroit bureau, carless and living in a downtown rooming house—in those years I was piling on "experiences" as fast, and often as recklessly, as I could.

Archibald MacLeish accepted me as a member of his workshop, which was top-of-the-line at Harvard. Although I was certainly outshone there, my inclusion did shine me up. By then I had some literary friends and had some idea of how things got written and what should become of them. But at graduation I was writing a hopelessly bad novel, a serious attempt which was not in the least intelligent or truly sentient. Several readers' reactions made it clear that I should pass onward.

I went to work for Texaco, in marketing, and eventually worked in what is now Ghana, Senegal, and the Ivory Coast, travelling on business through most of West Africa. There was reality, by God! The dynamics of colonial rule and exploitation, of African responses, of avarice and corruption on all sides were and are very plain to see.

While I was in Africa, Peter Matthiessen, a friend since our teens, took a short story, first written when I was at Harvard and much edited by him, for the second issue of the *Paris Review.* Released from Africa with a long paid leave, I started a novel, *A Far Place,* and got an advance on it from Mike Bessie at Harper. I quit Texaco, went to Paris to finish the book, and gravitated to the *Paris Review* office. Matthiessen and George Plimpton and the other founders had gone home, but Robert Silvers, now for many years editor of *The New York Review,* was in charge, and by lending him a hand as an unpaid assistant, I became an editor of the magazine.

So began a mostly literary life, writing, reading, and teaching. Only now at seventy-one do some of the truths I wanted to find about the society and family in which I grew up seem clear and interesting and worthy of sympathy.

Better, I think, for a young writer instinctively to feel that he or she knows the realities and sees through them to their ironies rather than, like me, to have struggled to pin down the real from the false. The struggle is likely to be rather humorless.

I came late to irony, but thank God I've got there. □

Somebody Almost Walked off wid all My Stuff

Jewelle Gomez

It started with listening. Listening to other people's stuff. To my great-grandmother, my grandmother, my father. The stories of their lives—as they were lived before there was me— unfolded around the kitchen table in the early hours of the morning and in the relaxed, smoky afterglow of holiday dinners. Perhaps it was because I wasn't being raised by my mother or father, or maybe their lives were really compelling, but for whatever reasons I'd hang on their words as if they were a radio play containing the secrets of the universe.

On cold New England nights in our draughty tenement apartment my great-grandmother and I would lean toward our big old radio to hear the melodramas of "The Shadow" or the Clay/Liston fight. The world was captured in that brown box behind knobs and lighted dials and made manifest just for us. I was mesmerized as the world spilled out across the scrubbed-clean oilcloth of our kitchen table like glittering treasure.

A similar force gripped me when I sat quietly, trying to be inconspicuous, while my mother and grandmother reminisced about their adventures as women-on-their-own in the more prosperous Boston of the forties and fifties. When my great-grandmother struggled with her memory to drag forth the life she'd known on Indian land in the Iowa of her youth, I captured any tiny detail she recovered. It seemed miraculous that the travesty of Indian life concocted for movie westerns could have an alternative reality embodied by the woman who combed my hair for school every morning.

And when I visited my father on the weekends and he regaled me into the late nights with stories of the patrons in the bar where he worked, I understood that the glamour and comedy of Hollywood movies had earthier counterparts in my own neighborhood. William Powell was a pale imitation of my father, Duke. Screen queens like Carole Lombard or Marilyn Monroe had stiff competition from the ladies of the evening who frequented my father's bar. And some, who were queens of a different sort, made Lana Turner seem a bit frumpy.

I looked forward to the stories my family and their friends told with an eagerness that bordered on compulsion. The magic of their memories was palpable as they floated in the air before me. I wanted to grab them, hold them close, feel their sweetness or salt against my skin.

At a point in my early adolescence the flow of energy shifted. I think I may have been standing around on the street corner, telling stories with other teenagers, a favorite pastime in my old neighborhood for those of us who didn't have the voices for doo-wop. We talked about school, our families, local gang activity, movies we'd seen; anything was the potential source of a joke. The laughter of my friends was always loud, encouraging. In this particular moment I understood that they were responding directly to me and my life, not to a tale I'd heard from someone else. I realized then that stories and a way of telling them was a gift I too might possess. My world did not have to be confined to absorbing the legends of my family's past. I had my own stuff.

   . . . this must be the spook house/another song
with no singers/lyrics/no voices/and interrupted
solos/unseen performances . . .

There is something just as destructive as living with the perpetual threat of violence, the desecration of your collective past, enduring the legal enforcement of your servitude and seeing society's conscious and unconscious dismissal of your humanity. That something is living and working through the Civil Rights and Black Power Movements, getting a taste of liberation from the horrors of the past, and then having your tongue cut out. After general enthusiasm for the Movements faded from the headlines and the public consciousness, a question remained: Who would want to hear the stories told by a raised-poor, colored lesbian? The answer—a very select few.

The response was a bitter taste in my mouth for more than a decade, choking me each time I stood near my typewriter.

I realized that I lived in a cultural system that is much more complex than black and white. All the reasons that black writers might be popular at a given moment didn't really apply to a colored lesbian writer or to one not writing about upward mobility, the trials of single parenthood, or drug addiction. I could not rely on those critics who'd been excited about the emergence of the voices like Gwendolyn Brooks, Amiri Baraka, Ishmael Reed, or Sonia Sanchez. My stuff did not feature me as a stately Dahomean queen ready to bear children for the nation or as a comic foil to nationalistic fantasies. My narratives sprang from the ethos of a fat little colored (that's what it said on my birth certificate) girl whose core impulse was to question everything. I kept imagining that I'd create a heroine like a bronze Mildred Pierce! Or that I'd be the contemporary James M. Cain, churning out sexy, provocative, political stories, kind of *noir* noire. Who would be interested in that, I wondered aloud? The silence that echoed back was as large as an overwrought storm cloud, casting a huge shadow over any effort I made.

I spent many hours at the typewriter steeped in the comedy and tragedy of trying to fit my life into the role models I watched on TV and in the movies: Me as Sandra Dee, Me as young and restless, Me as Miss Jane Pitman. The question of what I would write about was an empty koan, yielding no enlightenment.

Until the sixties, television was resolutely white, and I had participated in the colorization of the broadcasting universe when I worked for public TV and advocated "minority" inclusion. In the subsequent years I watched the airwaves flood with black characters from Cosby to Jimmy Walker to the Wayans—all comic, mostly male. They might as well have been Doris Day. I found little that resonated with my emotional life. In most cases, the writing was rudimentary, the characters simplistic, the concepts flat. After the struggle to get space on the airwaves, it was galling to see black life narrowed down to a laugh track. Were the people who laughed hysterically at JJ, then Martin, then "two snaps up," going to want to buy my stuff?

Trying to imagine my audience was nothing compared to the concomitant question: what to write about. I didn't see any indication anywhere that the people I knew or the things I thought about were of interest to anyone. In 1961, Lorraine Hansberry's play, *Raisin in the Sun,* was the first fissure in the blank wall I faced each time I thought about being a writer. The film version of her play, my initial encounter with the piece, was full of the energy and ideas I recognized from my own kitchen. At first it was simply invigorating to hear black voices and issues out loud in the world without a canned response behind them. But the film also made me cringe. The directorial emphasis was placed on the conflict between Walter Lee (who wanted to spend his father's insurance money on an ill-fated scheme) and his mother (who wanted the family to move to a better neighborhood). This subtly reduced the characters to reinforcements of gender stereotypes—the impetuous black man, the domineering black matriarch.

And more importantly for me, this interpretation obscured what I thought were Hansberry's more interesting questions: How do different generations and genders identify freedom? Could a woman (Ruth, Walter Lee's wife) maintain control over her own body and the right to abortion? Could a woman (Beneatha, his sister) insist on her right to an education above her duty to marry? Everywhere in the film the message was reinforced that tragedy is only significant when it befalls men. Of course, the musical version of the play, *Raisin*, erases the two women's crises completely!

Later, when I read the play, I was deeply moved, because it was the first time I'd read work by a black woman exploring the profoundly feminist issues I'd wrestled with since high school. I wanted to dance on my typewriter. But before the keys could be set to tapping, it occurred to me that in most of the public discussions of *Raisin in the Sun*, even the critics rarely mentioned the women's issues. The complications of women's lives were irrelevant in the literary (as well as the political) world. Black nationalists, colluding with the mainstream, dismissed Hansberry as middle class, as if most of them were not. I wanted to throw my typewriter through a window, preferably the window of one of the critics or nationalists. As sad as it made me, I realized that said critics were not always white and the nationalists were not always male. If the critical and political establishments couldn't recognize some truth from Lorraine Hansberry, would they ever even notice my work. The typewriter went flying through the window, my own window, and I was feeling a distinct chill.

For years afterward, each piece I started to write ended up in a small cardboard briefcase beneath piles of other useless pieces of paper. My first high school newspaper column, a love poem to a non-gender-specific inamorata, my personal response to Hansberry's work, all lay neatly stacked, turning brown. I would reread them occasionally just to see if there was anything of significance I hadn't discerned before. The ghostly hollow of my briefcase resounded, echoing back not a single word, idea, or impulse.

> I'm finally bein real/no longer symmetrical & impervious
>
> to pain. . .

In September 1976, I saw a production of Ntozake Shange's theatre piece, *For Colored Girls Who Have Considered Suicide when the Rainbow is Enuf*. I was twenty-eight, and my briefcase was bulging with empty, angry pages. At that moment and in the several times I returned to see what Shange described as a "choreopoem," I finally understood something about the impediments I felt looming over me. Like Shange, I wanted and needed to write about the women in my family, or the women that represented the things I cared about in life. But no one else seemed to place value on women's lives. Until I saw *For Colored Girls*, I'd never seen anything that put women at the center of the narrative so unashamedly. Each piece was about women and their response to the world around them. Women were active, not simply subjects. The whole presentation was balanced on the belief that black women had valuable lives that were of interest and whose experiences were of use to the broader world. Critical response to this notion in the black community was quite vitriolic. Yet each time I saw the choreopoem, I knew Shange was pointing me in the direction of a path through the brambles, moving me toward my work.

Each of the women on stage in Shange's piece told stories like those I'd heard in my kitchen and living room. They were the secrets girlfriends told each other on weekend sleepovers, whispered into the telephone, or wrote in their diaries. There were no easily digested laughs pumped up electronically or big tragic tears of victimization. There were complex poems full of insolence, sexuality, insecurity, sassiness, sadness, and sisterhood told in the unique voice of colored women. There were no neat endings and uncomplicated emotions for the women I knew, and there would be none in the stories I wrote, if I would dare to write them.

> I want my stuff back/my rythms & my voice/open my mouth/& let me
>
> talk ya outta/throwin' my shit in the sewar . . .

So I wrote a story about a lonely ghost, and a friend published it in an obscure college magazine. Then one about a lesbian only vampire that was published in a lesbian literary magazine, then some essays and some poems I published myself to avoid the agony of rejection. I started gathering my stuff together, all the pieces of myself that made up who I was and put them into the work. The Bostonian, journalist, left-handed, cinephile, colored, raised-poor, now middle class, teacher, lesbian, Trekkie, devotee of Streisand and Armatrading, and so on, all were part of the stories I would tell. In the late eighties, Audre Lorde, black lesbian writer and activist whose career spanned all the movements from the sixties to the present, encouraged me to publish my novel, *The Gilda Stories*. Several mainstream editors had rejected it with comments that the main character and premise were too complex. But Audre, through the example of her own life and philosophy as well as in explicit discussion, assured me that it was that complexity within myself that would make the writing important. She crystallized all that I'd gleaned from Shange's work and the responses to it.

Eventually, in 1996, my stage adaptation of my novel toured the United States performed by Urban Bush Women, an internationally known performance company. There was almost no day during the two years I worked on the script that I didn't think of Shange's choreopoem, its success, and the attacks against its women-centered premise. My piece featured colored lesbians and I braced myself to be excoriated as she'd been and as Alice Walker had been a decade later when she dared to write her novel, *The Color Purple*.

The brickbats were not hurled, at least not in the same way. Instead, reviewers mostly ignored the lesbian aspect of the characters, as well as the meaning of the story itself and focused on the (fabulous) dancing. Still, it was with Shange and Walker in my mind that I was able to keep pushing forward to finish the work, and the spirit of their stuff hung out there on the stage with mine.

It seems suspiciously easy to be able to pinpoint a specific epiphany—Shange's production—as so pivotal in my ability and inspiration to write. But more than twenty years after that event I can still feel the tingling moment of recognition and remember the weight of silence lifting from me.

Today, if I ask myself who'll read about the women I write

about the answer is the same—precious few. Mainstream reviewers rarely look at books by independent presses, especially if the writer or protagonists are black and lesbian, no matter what the topic or genre. Even success (continued high sales of my fiction, sold-out audiences for my play, etc.) doesn't inspire publishers and producers to rush in with offers for a black lesbian writer. The educational system, the critical hierarchy and cultural arbiters, continue to assume that my life and work are not of interest to the "general" reader. But the audience for my writing remains devoted, loyal, and varied. Just as I found myself enraptured by the personal history my family unfolded, there are others with the same hunger for the new worlds of the past and the imagination of the future.

I no longer worry about what my subject will be when I sit down to write. I had the good fortune to come into the world in a family that honored the stories it had to share and at a time when the social movements inspired an urgency for those stories. I have enough people of all types in my family and in my head to populate several worlds.

I'm more concerned that I might not have enough hours, between a full-time job and creeping middle age, to finish all the projects that percolate inside me. I don't even worry as much about who'll read what I write. As long as independent presses can survive, I can drum up enough people to buy copies of my books. Of course, I'd love to be the toast of the town, with glowing reviews, writing awards, book and film contracts stuffed and mounted on my mantelpiece. Almost everybody, especially a writer, wants approval.

But mostly I just try to keep up with "alla my stuff," so I don't lose track of it or devalue it before I can get it down on the page. And I keep listening to other people's stuff. □

THE VISITOR

Forrest Hamer

She and I hadn't gotten along in a long while. Before the fire, she would appear just before day, rocking in an old chair that wasn't there, and wait for me to say something. Later, we developed what might be called a way of conversing— I'd look toward her and listen, I'd whisper back; and no one, not even someone lying next to me, could say they ever heard a thing.

She had a lot to talk about: She was the woman I'd seen years before in a book on slavery, her naked back facing out, all kinds of scars where she'd been whipped, and, at the right hip, her hand. I'd seen the photograph not long after the Fisk Jubilee Singers had passed through town, giving a concert at our church. Most people in the congregation favored the gospel music, especially the faster tempo songs stirred along by a new electric organ capable of singing in chorus by itself, but I was haunted by the slave songs the college students had sung a cappella, by some uncomfortable past I heard in the amens of old folks who otherwise wanted no part of talk about the slavery days. I was respectful, but their silence intrigued me. When I saw the picture of that woman, I already knew what she sounded like singing; she seemed even more willing to speak.

It wasn't until I'd left the South, though, that she began making her visits. To my own surprise and to the delight of my musically talented family, I'd joined a gospel choir in college—me who'd been always too shy to sing out loud, who'd been so eager to leave behind the family expectations that I would attend church each Sunday *at least once.* But I moved away only to find singing necessary that far away from home, and I enjoyed the Sunday morning and Wednesday evening times of song.

In my second year of college, I became so restless I wanted to leave my life and go wandering. I didn't know where and I couldn't say why, but I just became *dissatisfied*. My adolescent ambition to become a writer had become oppressive—it was harder and harder to finish anything, and I felt my new experiences outstripped the language I had to describe them. I also didn't like the way I knew myself; I struggled toward and against a racial identity, my sexuality, and what I could see as my own peculiar history. I lost interest in classes, I stopped going to choir practice, and all I wanted was the courage to leave. She began her visits.

She warned me some folks wander away never to come back. She warned me of the failure my dropping out of college would represent to kin present and past. She warned me I'd still feel restless even when I arrived where I'd be going. And she began telling me of children she'd lost, the ones sold away from her, dispersed who knew where. I could help her find them if I stayed right where I was. I could help her find them if I waited.

But waiting got to be too much for me. I stopped writing altogether, and my restlessness grew painful. Finally, in some destructive act of creativity, I took all the pages of poems and half-poems, the not-completed dialogues of plays, all the stories I'd written and was writing, and I quickly burned them up. I decided then to abandon writing and find some other way of staying involved with subjective life while also being in the world. I decided to become a psychologist. For a while, a decade almost, this compromise worked. I went to graduate school. I left writing to other people. I would envy them, even as I sought those who wrote what I longed to read.

In the beginning, she would still come, but she was angry. As if I'd put her in that fire. As if I'd denied her. At times, I'd look to see her rocking in that chair and I wanted her to leave me alone. Her railing annoyed me, the hurt in the songs she sang seemed just too much. At other times, I'd think to ask her something else about the history she'd taught me. Maybe I could serve her as a generously educated man, or perhaps even as a psychologist. Maybe I could support others more qualified and gifted to write about her. Maybe they would be more loyal. But she said less and less, and, after a bit, she even stopped visiting. And I stopped looking for her.

Becoming a psychologist seemed mostly incompatible with creative writing, anyway. Graduate school was consuming. I was being trained to attempt some illusory objectivity about human motives and behavior, to develop and test hypotheses about them, all in the service of being helpful. And when I then began to train as a psychotherapist, I gave my working attention to people facing differing life problems, to being supervised myself, and to assuming an identity that is a culture all its own.

Except I wasn't finishing my dissertation. Except I couldn't sustain caring about a project I knew to be only another long paper, only an exercise. And when I finally—and slowly—confronted with the help of a good analyst the reasons behind this surprising lack of love, I was faced again with my self. I was faced with what I had so callously abandoned and left back East or down South. And, aside from the anxiety about going further educationally than anyone in my family had ever gone, about possibly losing my connection to the people I still loved most in the world, I was afraid I'd come to lack feeling connected to anyone at all. For it was a measure of solitude I feared most, the solitude most writers need and frankly love. The very solitude wherein real conversations with imaginary companions finally take place.

I became less afraid of solitude only gradually, and only with a lot of reassuring myself that I could maintain some sense of being the same. I became less engaged with some of the people in my life, as well as with many of the distractions I had so keenly cultivated. And I became more engaged with the academic writing that finally took only a few months to complete. During this era, I found myself thinking of a play I'd started just before I tried to burn everything up. It was set during a choir practice and the characters included voices I'd listened to as a child. I also thought about the woman I'd not thought much about for years. I promised myself I would try someday to write that play.

She had returned to my life, then. She was still angry, and she didn't seem to trust me. She'd appear for a few minutes, be gone for weeks or months, come back for just as long. When she was with me, she railed more and she ranted. Her story had now become particular—a son who'd been sold away was someone I might know, if only I'd be loyal. And though she seemed to appreciate being made real again, she said she didn't know that I wouldn't become violent with myself again. She would stay as long as it took to finish the dissertation; afterwards, she'd just have to see. In turn, I took to arguing back, defensively angry at being portrayed as a coward, but wary of the scope of her requirements.

For a couple of years, I took on clinical work to provide more professional training, as well as to begin paying off my huge debts. On the weekends, sometimes in transit between places of work, I would try to make a place inside myself where writing might happen, where I could envision myself as a writer. The construction was slow going, because there were so many professional involvements that also interested me.

On my thirty-third birthday, I became convinced I would not live through the year. The allusion to Christian history amused me, but I was also frightened. I kept the feeling secret. I didn't acknowledge to my friends how my prospective death had elaborated itself and how I imagined it as sudden, violent, and pointless. I made contingency plans. I became less attached to the idea of a future. I even took comfort in the smallness of one life relative to the vastness of generations. But I was more and more restless, and by the end of that year, when I heard Peggy Lee sing, over and over, "Is that all there is," I itched once again to get on.

The move I was faced with making was now more clearly internal. Moving back East, or moving overseas, even moving to live near my aging parents were possibilities I considered, but, as the woman had said to me some years ago: Some people wander away never to come back. During this time, I was more aware of her presence, much more aware of how I was able to call to her. I admitted that I had tried to kill her, and I accepted that awesome responsibility. In one memorable conversation, she asked me about my life: Did I want to live a contented life? A good life? Did I even want to live at all? If I decided to live, she implied, I could not do so without also deciding to write.

I decided to live. I decided I would wait with the ever-present threat of being mute, or being silenced by the reactions of others. I decided I would learn to sit still and write and write and write until I wrote myself away.

I also decided I would speak of and from what I might call my own life. I decided I would finally reveal myself to those who had come before me, among them the woman who'd come alive once more in my life. Maybe there could be some peace.

I've thought of her less and less. We trust each other more. Periodically, I have to make my decision all over again. Periodically, I decide once more to face the possibility of deciding to die. It happens in various ways—becoming depressed, losing interest in what matters most to me, becoming simply afraid. Usually, I recognize the chance to thrive. And, usually, I want to live. □

FINDING THE TRAP DOOR

Adam Hochschild

*U*nlike other animals, writers are not born into the world knowing how to make their own particular noise. Almost from the beginning, wolves howl, hogs grunt, bears growl. They, need no MFA programs in growling, or summer workshops in discovering the grunt within. Even if separated from their families at birth and raised by some other species, they still know the right sound. But writers are different: all too easily they mistake someone else's sound for their own. For many years, that's what happened with me.

Ever since I could remember, I had wanted to write novels. As a child I loved reading them; when I went away to boarding school at age thirteen, a fine freshman English teacher helped me hear the chords and echoes that could lie below the surface of a piece of fiction. One day he gave me an extra-credit assignment to write about a couple of short stories. One was John Galsworthy's "The Apple Tree." It's the story of all upper-class Englishman, out hiking in the country, who falls in love with a beautiful Welsh farm girl. He swears eternal devotion, and promises to come back to the farm so they can elope. But then he is seduced back into his usual social world, fails to return to the farm, and soon marries a conventional woman of his own class. Years later, he learns that the farm girl killed herself in grief, and sees that his own life has been wasted.

I was at an age where I wanted every story to have a message, and the moral of this one was, to me, crystal clear. The conventional life was the life of a lawyer or businessman that parents, teachers, and family friends seemed to assume I would lead. The radiantly beautiful farm girl was the alluring alternative: my life as a writer of fiction. Unlike that of the hero of the story, I vowed, my life would not be wasted. I would make the right choice.

Despite the English teacher who inadvertently helped awaken these ideas, my New England prep school came to feel like part of that constricting circle of others' expectations that I needed to escape. Harvard felt even more so, so great was my restlessness. The English courses I took there only strengthened my assumption that the greatest of human achievements was to write novels. I was eager to be finished with formal education and to enter the real world beyond. I came West, and in 1965 I began working as a reporter for the *San Francisco Chronicle*. Hadn't journalism been the route toward literature for Hemingway, for Stephen Crane? I hoped it would be the same for me.

I was now beginning to write short stories, and most of them were set in various down-and-out milieux I was seeing as a reporter. I was constantly racing to the scene of fires, robberies, murders, and suicides. Working in a newspaper city room in those preelectronic days was noisy and exciting. You banged away on a manual typewriter. Near deadline, a copy boy stood by to run each page of your story, the moment you finished it, to the city desk. Overhead, pneumatic tubes whooshed and thumped as they carried copy and proofs to and from the composing room. On the wall, a bell connected to the San Francisco Fire Department's alarm system clanged away, and the moment it gave the *ding-ding, ding-ding* signal for a second alarm, a reporter and a photographer began running for a car. On the city desk, a police radio poured forth an unending static-laden litany of woe and disaster. One afternoon, listening to it, the city editor, a small man with a big voice and suspenders, suddenly rose in his seat, pointed at me, and bellowed, "Hochschild! There's a woman having a baby in a taxi! Go!" I was so rattled when I got to the scene that, amazingly, I didn't even notice whether the baby was a boy or a girl. But I was happy: This was the real world at last, in all its gritty glory, soon to be immortalized in my fiction.

Besides experience in journalism, there were other classic, ingredients to being a successful young novelist, I knew from my reading and my college courses. One of them I could not meet: if possible, you should be from a poor background, like Chekhov or Dreiser. Alas, my family was distressingly well-off. My father, with whom I had a tense and difficult relationship, was the retired CEO of a multinational mining corporation. More frustrating yet, in my rebellion against him I couldn't feel that I was the voice of my generation, of sons against fathers during this tumultuous decade of upheavals over the civil rights movement and Vietnam. He was remarkably liberal, as opposed to the Vietnam War as I.

However, my parents were at least out of sight, on the other side of the country. I seldom talked about them with my friends, and would not have dreamed, in what I wrote, of revealing much about the world I had come from. One of the few people who knew was my wife, Arlie, then a graduate student, later to become a professor at Berkeley and a superb writer of social science with an artist's eye. She and I lived, if not in Chekhovian poverty, at least in conspicuous simplicity. We drove a VW Beetle, and our threadbare furniture came from the Salvation Army store.

At home, I was not doing my fiction writing in a proper Paris garret, above a brothel or sawmill (like Hemingway's apartment), but I had almost the equivalent. Our two-room apartment was in a pleasant but slightly dilapidated brown-shingle building in Berkeley, and underneath the glassed-in sun porch in back, where I wrote, the ground had subsided. The floor slanted, and at first pencils rolled away from me on the top of my Salvation Army desk. I had to saw an inch and a half off the two near legs to make the desktop level.

After some two years of newspaper work, I moved on to a job editing and writing at *Ramparts*. But my articles there, like my unpublished short stories, were in my mind only steps toward the big breakthrough, my first novel. I planned one out, and wrote several chapters and an outline of what was to come. Miraculously, in 1969 a New York publisher gave me a contract and a $5,000 advance ($20,000 in today's money). I was deliriously happy. Still in my mid-twenties, I was on my way. My career—my real career—was launched.

By now I was no longer working at *Ramparts*. When people asked me what I did, I loved saying that I was writing a novel. This gave me an identity, and in a strange way I think I cared about that most of all. My writing felt important, of course, but as I look back at it now, I think it was important to me mainly as a vehicle for my being able to think of myself as a writer. I got occasional offers of freelance magazine assignments, but I turned most down: I was doing my novel, and almost anything else, I felt, would be something lesser. Would Proust or Tolstoy have paused to write a profile or a book review?

When anyone asked what my novel was about, I said, enigmatically, that I preferred not to talk about it. I knew, from reading *Paris Review* interviews, that we real writers seldom described works-in-progress. The creative process was complex and delicate, and could easily be disturbed by insensitive questions from ordinary mortals. For the same reason, as I worked, I showed the manuscript to almost no one.

I imagined my own *Paris Review* interview some years hence. I would talk about the major literary influences on me, about my adventurous newspaper days, and about the big breakthrough of my, first novel, after which it was all smooth sailing. I would have some wise words of advice for younger writers. And then I would wait for the interviewer to notice the slanting floor and the sawed-off desk legs.

I worked on the novel steadily. One of the few times I wrote something else was to spend a couple of days jotting down some childhood memories that bubbled up with unexpected insistency when an uncle of mine died. He was a swashbuckling Russian who had been a fighter pilot in the First World War. He had worked his way through Europe as an opera singer, flown explorers around Africa, and then shocked everyone in the family by marrying my father's shy, staid sister. But however colorful and vibrant a presence he had been to me as a boy, he was a figure from another era, an ardent Tsarist to the day of his death, who seemed to have nothing to do with the American rebels of the sixties whose literary voice I hoped to be. I filed those pages away at the back of a drawer and forgot about them.

After several years, I finished the novel and mailed it off. I waited for the praise I was sure would come when my editor read the full manuscript for the first time. Then came a terrible blow. The editor told me he did not want to publish it. It had never occurred to me that this might happen. Didn't I have a contract, an advance already paid? More important still, hadn't I been telling, people for several years now that I was a novelist? I felt like a groom abandoned at the altar when the wedding guests are already seated, the organist is already playing. I was crushed. My editor, I was sure, had committed a felony against American literature.

I showed the manuscript to other publishers. No luck. I tried sending it around in England—hadn't Joyce also been spurned by small-minded publishers in his own country? No luck there, either. There was a recession in the publishing industry, I told friends; there were mergers, acquisitions, dark forces at work; it's harder than ever for decent books to get published these days. . . .

Worst of all, after a gap of many despairing months, I reread my manuscript once again and began to see why no one wanted to print it. I had followed all the rules—the prose sparkled, the generations clashed, the stream-of-consciousness passages were all in lower-case italics, the symbols coyly awaited discovery by alert critics—but the characters were stiff and one-dimensional. The novel lacked the sound of a human voice.

Chastened, with a sense of having wasted several years, I went back to what I had thought of as my lower-ranking trade, journalism. In 1974, some friends and I started *Mother Jones*. I contributed to the new venture some of my family's ill-gotten gains I had inherited, and, with surprising ease, we raised much more money elsewhere. We were lucky in our timing, for it was in the wake of Watergate and the country was ready for a new magazine with an anti-Establishment, investigative edge.

Fortunately, I had colleagues who knew how to run the business side of things, and I was able to concentrate on being an editor. Unexpectedly, I found myself learning something enormously valuable from this work. The job demystifies words. It reminds you, as you look at letters to the editor and reader surveys and listen to what subscribers tell you, that readers are impatient and busy. You have to compete for their attention. Is this article going to keep someone reading for six thousand words? Or is it worth only two thousand? Or should we drop it entirely—even if it was written by an old friend, a famous writer, or one of us? Whether it's an exposé, a piece of reportage, or a short story, you learn that no piece of writing is sacred. The reader, not the writer, comes first. And nothing has value just because *you* wrote it.

During those years as an editor I wrote very little, still nagged by a lingering sense of my previous failure. Every once in a while, I would skim through the manuscript of my old novel, and humiliation would wash over me once more.

Eventually I began writing again, although only about one longer article a year. At first these were, like most of what we ran in *Mother Jones*, political commentary or investigative reporting. I was dimly aware, though, that others could do this better than I. Then quite a different sort of idea came to me.

For several years I had been admiring the books of Victor Serge. Serge was a Belgian-born anarchist who fought with the Bolsheviks in the Russian Civil War. He spoke out for free speech and democracy, and was harassed, jailed, and sent into internal exile by Stalin. He finally managed to get out of the Soviet Union in 1936, published several novels, and then, a few years later, had to flee to Mexico one step ahead of the Gestapo. Suddenly, rereading Serge's memoirs, I realized that on one day in October 1919, at the site of an old observatory just outside Petrograd, Victor Serge and my beloved Russian uncle, Boris Sergievsky, had fought on opposite sides of the very same battle. I decided to write about these two men who each stood for something so different.

In 1978 I went to Russia, found the battlefield, searched out places where each man had lived, and enjoyed the puzzled reaction of Russians to my strange quest. Once home I wrote the article, and found myself feeling a kind of inner satisfaction I had not known before. It was not a sense that I had written anything great or lasting. Rather, I merely felt that for the first time in my life, I had written something in my own voice. Almost everything else — the other magazine and newspaper articles, the unpublished novel and short stories — was, I now saw, in one way or another in someone else's voice.

My voice was not what I had expected. It seemed like a long-lost identical twin, who turned out not to look like what I thought I looked like. For one thing, it had none of the rhetorical flourishes or instantly recognizable style of some of my favorite novelists. For another, this voice of mine was not writing novels at all, but nonfiction.

As I think about it now, what seemed to have coaxed my voice out of me and brought it to life this first time was a coming together of three things. One was the chance to examine some contradictory feelings — my admiration for these two men who had once been trying to kill each other. Another was leaping back and forth in time, between the Russian Revolution and my travels sixty years later. Is there anything more exhilarating than time-traveling? And finally, I was writing about people I cared about. Why, I now wonder, in my previous fifteen years of writing, had I almost never done any of these things before?

Not long after this, as I was nearing my fortieth birthday, my father died. Much of my life, and my very becoming a writer, which had at first disturbed him greatly, had been a sort of quiet rebellion against his hopes and plans for me. And now he was no longer there. It's as if you spend all your life with one hand braced against a wall that threatens to topple over on you. Then suddenly one day the wall vanishes. It is hard to find your balance.

At this time I was also feeling burned out from doing magazine editing for the better part of a decade. I still had that persistent dream that my real work was as a novelist. And so in 1981 I left my job as an editor and spent some months working on a new novel. But like the first it felt wooden and lifeless. At least I was now self-aware enough to see this and give it up.

I felt all roads were blocked. As a last resort, I decided to work on a memoir. Writing one was something I had long thought about, but was sure I wouldn't do for years. Most novelists, after all, seem to write their autobiographies at the end of their fiction-writing careers. I think this is because they are wary of disclosing too much about their real worlds while they are still trying to catch readers up in imaginary ones. For me, with the privileged background I had spent much energy in avoiding mentioning, this seemed to be especially true. And so the memoir I had sometimes imagined, finally revealing some information about my private life to a surprised world, was supposed to be a late, minor appendage to my career as a novelist. It felt all wrong to be doing it first.

But I was stuck. I had nothing else I felt able to write. I figured I would write this book, then put the manuscript away for some years. I would try to publish it only after I had produced those novels which, I hoped, were still somewhere inside me.

To my great surprise, the memoir came tumbling out quickly. Telling myself that I wouldn't try to publish it right away had mysteriously opened a lock. Writing the book barely felt like work, more like writing a letter to a friend. To my further surprise, I realized that I had long ago written the opening pages: those childhood memories of my Uncle Boris, quickly jotted down and filed away a decade earlier, then used more recently in that article from Russia. I finished a rough draft of the book in two-and-a-half months.

I revised the manuscript, and showed it to friends. In the preceding fifteen years I had learned this: forget all that coy concealment about work-in-progress in those *Paris Review* interviews. Talking about a piece of writing, trying it out on people, seeing where they get interested and where they get bored, is the most precious tool a writer has. If a piece of writing doesn't have the effect on people you want, then you can go back and try again. That's a luxury that an airplane designer or bridge engineer doesn't have.

One day I realized I had abandoned another earlier belief as well. While continuing to revise my memoir I was, I noticed, doing more other kinds of writing than ever: magazine and op-ed pieces, a book review column for *Mother Jones*, a regular commentary for National Public Radio. At bedtime, I found I was telling my children stories, with a regular stable of oddball characters. Sometimes we would take turns, each carrying the story a lap further. Instead of distracting me from my book, all these things seemed to help, as if limbering up some additional literary muscles I hadn't known about before. By accident, I had learned that each of us does not have just one voice, but many, and that speaking in one of them can help bring the others to life. "Any proper writer ought to be able to write anything," Kingsley Amis once said, "from an Easter Day sermon to a sheep-dip handout."

My feeling of not wanting to publish the memoir for a long time evaporated, replaced by the simple vanity of wanting to publish it now. It would not, after all, be the life story of a famous novelist, only of a human being. *Half the Way Home: a Memoir of Father and Son* was published by Viking Penguin in 1986 and stayed in print, with one or two short breaks, until last year; it will shortly be reprinted by Syracuse University Press. I've written several more books since then, but *Half the Way Home* was a turning point that made it possible for me to go forward.

Two unexpected things happened after the book appeared. The first occurred a year or so later. The excitement of getting good reviews had dissipated. I was stalled in my next book. And so I did what I had always done when feeling low: I pulled out the manuscript of my first novel, so as to feel a failure once again for having wasted all that time. But as I now read through it something struck me like a thunderclap. The manuscript was, I saw, a first version of *Half the Way Home*. True, it was a novel, not a memoir. The main character was a young woman, not me. Her parents were largely not my parents. The house she grew up in was smaller, and in a different part of the country. But the underlying feelings I was trying to evoke—clumsily and unsuccessfully this first time round—were the same. Like some biographer poking through his subject's attic, I had discovered my own first draft. So: all that time and effort had not been wasted after all. I felt as if an enormous burden had been lifted from me.

The other interesting thing that has happened since *Half the Way Home* appeared is this: When I run into people who have read the book, or get letters from them, sometimes they begin by saying, I read your novel. . . ." At first, my impulse was always to correct people, to say that the book is clearly labeled a memoir, that I didn't make anything up, that it's all true. Today I am more bemused. Slips of the memory reveal something, like slips of the tongue. What I think the "I read your novel" shows is that we are accustomed to turning to nonfiction books for information, and to novels for character and emotion. After all, isn't this exactly what I had believed for years—thinking that if I wanted to portray a character, to make a reader feel, I could only do so by writing novels?

Now I feel much more relaxed about all this. The important thing is to evoke those feelings and to make those characters live and breathe and walk off the page, whether you're writing fiction, nonfiction, or something in between. Often the right form turns out to be something entirely different than what you had once imagined. My own, it appears, usually seems to be some mixture of history and first-person reportage, and the more leaps between them the better. And characters are everything. Searching for good ones and for the meanings embodied in their lives has taken me, physically or intellectually, to some times and places I wouldn't have missed for anything: to South Africa in the early nineteenth century and in the late 1980s; to remote corners of Siberia in the Stalin years and today; and, for a book I'm working on now, to the Congo in the time of Joseph Conrad and King Leopold II. Amazingly, I actually get paid for doing this. It sure beats writing about the world of the San Francisco police beat.

Sometimes I think of being a writer as like being a would-be singer, ready to give a concert, who is trapped in a pitch-black house. The lights are off, the doors are closed; unexpected screens and barriers stand everywhere; floor-length blackout curtains cover all the windows. You stumble around in the dark, banging into things, shouting but not heard. You have only a limited amount of time—that's what life is, after all—and in it you have to find the magical opening, the window or door through which you can stick out your head and sing, so that those outside can hear you at last.

Bumping about in the darkness, most of us tend to grope toward the traditional grand aperture: those French windows of the novel. Find them, fling them open, and there you are on the balcony, ready to sing your song. There are other traditional openings, too: the smaller window of the short story, the doorway of the poem.

But now, I am beginning to see, there are all sorts of other ways out of the darkened house as well, and all of them let the light in and your voice out: dormer windows, a little wicket for the meter-reader, skylights that swing open, chimneys you can stick your head up, the secret trap door hidden under the rug. Some day, perhaps, I'll stumble upon those French windows and write a novel. If not, I won't be disappointed. Recently, I have found myself writing very short stories for very small children. My kids have now grown up, and those stories simply need somewhere to go. What passage out of the house is this analogous to? Maybe to that little flap the cat pushes through to get in and out of the backyard. In any case, it's something that won't be found by someone looking only for the French windows. To me it feels like a real opening out of the house, nonetheless. I plan to keep looking for more. □

Putting Aside My Fears

Ginu Kamani

*T*oward the end of 1995, my thirteen-year-old stepson came home from the music store with some audiocassettes. Not having followed popular music for some years now, I don't recognize any of the bands he follows, so I thought nothing of his new tapes. A few days later I found them on top of the stereo and picked them up out of curiosity. To my astonishment, the tapes were compilations of disco music from the seventies. I could not believe it. My pulse quickening, I checked the song titles and recognized every single one, including favorites by Thelma Houston, Diana Ross, K. C. & the Sunshine Band, Van McCoy. . . . I was ecstatic. After making sure I was alone, I blasted the music at deafening volume and danced until exhausted and drenched in sweat.

So what does that have to do with how I became a writer?

Developing into a writer was only possible because disco music warded off the dark forces that might have crushed my spirit irrevocably.

Let me explain.

As a child in Bombay, I lived in a virtual children's paradise, growing up with numerous cousins and playmates. All I remember of my free time in childhood was the delight of play, play, and more play. The introverted side of myself wasn't in evidence then at all.

Childhood ended the moment puberty hit, too hard and too early in my case. My world was turned upside down. My body, which had been washed, dressed, and fussed over for years by women servants, was suddenly passed into my own care. I didn't know this body. I hadn't even noticed the gradual changes that should have become abundantly clear in the middle of my tenth year: the growing breasts, the rounded hips, the dense body hair. I was instructed by my mother and other female adults that I now had to watch my dress, my speech, and my actions in public. I could no longer engage in childish activities with abandon.

I was outraged. I didn't understand anything about my new form. I didn't like tending to its needs. I stuck out prominently in a class full of bony, pre-pubescent girls. I withdrew into myself. Life changed completely.

A year later, in 1974, when my family visited the U.S., I got hooked on pop music. I remained glued to the radio for the entire trip. Stevie Wonder was big that summer, as were Marie Osmond, *Grease*, and the first stirrings of disco.

Upon my return to India, the short-wave radio became my constant companion. With my ear to the transistor, I heard all the latest hits in the West long before (if ever) they reached record stores in India. BBC World Service, Radio Kuwait, Voice of America, Radio Sri Lanka, Radio Nederland.

In those years, we had a record player and a reel-to-reel at home, and my father had a highly coveted eight-track in his car. In 1975, in a big move, my father replaced the eight-track with an audiocassette player. From somewhere, we kids got hold of Donna Summer's "Love To Love You, Baby" on cassette. There was only one place to play it. I still remember the scene of my father's car crammed full of teenagers with Donna Summer blasting out of quad speakers in the mid-day Bombay heat. The driver of my father's car hung around nervously, haranguing us about the potential damage we were doing to the vehicle in his charge.

Donna Summer became the presiding goddess of my domestic realm. Someone graciously taped her LP onto reel-to-reel, and even with the player situated in the most public part of the house I recall plugging in the earphones and dancing right there in the living room as wildly as I could manage without being yanked back by the restraining leash of the connecting wire. The bemused servants kept walking through the room, grinning and staring as I wiggled with such urgency. It was a matter of some concern that as a member of a good family I appeared to have lost my poise and inhibitions so completely.

1976. We were just a few months from leaving India permanently, but I didn't know it as yet. I was glued to the radio night and day. I kept a journal of what songs the foreign stations played. I was thirteen, but, to my utter delight, passed for eighteen and was allowed in with my (also underage) older sister to Bombay's only disco at that time, Blow Up, in the five-star Taj Mahal Hotel. After hearing the latest dance music with constant static for so long, the real thing pulsing in my ears and under my feet was irresistible. Somewhat less appealing were the pulsing items owned by overly eager male dance partners, but that wasn't half as revolting as being kissed full on the mouth by the older uncle of a friend. Yeccchhh!

In August of 1976, my family left India under cover of darkness. My father's family business had been completely destroyed due to in-fighting, and my father was fleeing for his life and the safety of the family.

In retrospect, I'm sure I was just as shell-shocked as any other immigrant could expect to be. However, what insulated me initially were elaborate fantasies about America being the only place worthy of me and my dreams. I was very excited by the prospect of going to a mixed American high school, given my years in all-girls schools. I didn't begin high school until November of that year. I had three months in which to imagine what a cool place high school would be. Unhappily, I was wrong. From my very first day I went into withdrawal.

My peers clearly had no interest in me and I was not interested in them. Not only did I look weird, but I spoke weird and dressed weird. I was also a straight-A student from the start. I was horrified by the pressures to appear deliberately stupid—a minimal requisite for peer approval. I was dumbfounded by the attitudes that studies were worthless, and that sex, fashion, smoking, and drinking were the only real priorities for the future.

My strategy for dealing with this dystopia was to return home in the afternoons and lock myself in a room with the radio on and dance to disco music until I was exhausted. For hours at a stretch I lost my mind and body in that world completely. The issue was not simply one of separating myself physically from people I didn't trust, or of needing to be alone while adjusting to new pressures; it was about having an intense, sensual, and highly pleasurable means of release, which coincidentally soothed away the daily accumulation of anxieties, rejections, and blunders. I see it as my version of a holding pattern, while I nurtured my certainty that I was meant for something special in life, without yet having the faintest idea of how, when, or where. While I waited, disco dancing kept my spirits high.

The habit of locking myself up and dancing to the radio persisted all the way through high school, into college, through my first live-in relationship, right through the end of my B.A. Eight years in total, from the time my family moved to the U.S. I recall a few uneasy moments as disco began to die out in the early eighties: at a college social the DJ blasted AC/DC over the speakers, and to my horror people actually rushed onto the floor. But with Michael Jackson and Madonna cranking out hits, synth dance music picked up where disco left off. I was well provided for until 1985 when, as a consequence of preparing for my entry into the M A. program, this part of my life phased out entirely. I was ready to write.

Disco music had helped protect me from becoming depressed, paralyzed, fearful, schizophrenic, ill at ease with my identity, self-destructive, self-hating, vapid, defeated. What grew within me in that protected period was a deeply felt sensuality, a comfort with the excitability and pleasures of the body, the ability to seek out forms of release from potentially disabling pressures, long internal dialogues, and extensive intellectual activity, curiosity and interest in my personal processes, a capacity for black humor, and the self-assurance to reject people and ideas that disturbed my personal sanctity.

My introversion gave way in the M.A. program to solidly backed opinions, good writing skills, and a penchant for the mysteries of human relationships. In my writing I returned full-scale to the memories of my years in India, and at the end of the program I returned to India in person, reconnecting with the culture once again as a capable, creative adult.

Some time back I was informed by a woman writer of South Asian descent that she loved my story "Waxing the Thing" and wished she could write like that, but knew that if she ever took on similar topics, her family would turn on her full force. She had managed to write until then without ruffling their feathers, and felt no permission to test their limits or take them on about the ways in which they might be restricting her. She continued to write with self-censorship as her guiding star, unable to express herself the way she yearned to.

The anger of family and community loom large in the

imaginations of Indians, debilitating superegos that stop most of us dead in our tracks. I tried to imagine being in her position, but I could not. I have yet to restrain myself from writing anything because of the potential response of family or community. Somewhere, somehow, I have managed to secure that most elusive of credentials: permission—to look, to touch, to explore, to analyze, to question, to invent, to express. Without permission I could never have become the person my younger self was waiting to turn into, or the writer that I am.

The fear of fear is a Catch-22 that sucks the spirit with the force of a hurricane. When I look back, I marvel at how the impulse to utilize music and dance allowed me to put aside my fears, to trust my instincts, to turn on my senses, and to play. □

GIRL POET

Dorianne Laux

I came to poetry as a girl through the pages of a novel called *A Tree Grows in Brooklyn* by Betty Smith. Published in 1943, I probably read it around twenty years later, when I was eleven years old. I was completely taken with the story of Francie Nolan, whose first name was the same as my mother's and I liked to imagine my mother as a young girl similar to the one I read about. I didn't merely like the book and its characters, I loved them: Francie, a bookish and introspective girl with an out-of-work Irish father who drank too much, a younger brother who was always in trouble, a beautiful and hardworking mother, and a flamboyant and funny aunt who couldn't have children, all of them living in the gritty brick tenements of Brooklyn. I cherished Francie like a sister, like the mother whose childhood was a mystery to me, like the woman I wanted to become. I think what I appreciated most about Francie was that she was willing to reveal herself, to disclose quietly and without self-pity the harsh facts of her life.

Francie's reality was so unlike my own that I perceived her to be exotic. I entered Francie's world like any good reader would, and, more importantly, she entered mine. I learned things from her that others had tried to teach me but failed. I was schooled by example to be strong, tenacious, and honest, hardworking and watchful, curious, brave, and true. I learned when it was prudent to be silent and wise to speak up, why to listen and where to look, how to think, and even how to feel. I re-read *A Tree Grows in Brooklyn* at least once a year, every year, from the time I was eleven until well after high school. I memorized poetic passages and recited them to myself before falling asleep. I made the chapter about Francie and her brother dragging home a free Christmas tree into a monologue for my drama class. I read a page about the meal the Nolan family had on Thanksgiving to my family on Thanksgiving as a new kind of prayer. Years later I would read selections to the children at my local library for story hour, and, even later, to my own daughter at bedtime. Francie Nolan had become an inextricable part of my spirit. She was the companion of my childhood who would never leave me, a familiar I could count on, a friend who would never die.

I was probably thirteen, when, one day, after re-reading the book again, I tried my hand at a number of poems. Dissatisfied with most but delighted with one, I read it aloud to myself a few times before hiding the batch under my bed. As I lay there daydreaming, I suddenly realized that Francie was not Francie, but rather a character invented by a writer, a real woman living somewhere in the world whose name was Betty Smith. The book I had then and still own was published by The Blakiston Company in Philadelphia. On the copyright page the publication date was written in Roman numerals. It was stated that this edition was made by special arrangement with Harper & Brothers in New York. But nowhere, front or back, did the book reveal anything about its author. And so I was free to make her up.

From then on, I liked to imagine Smith writing her book enthroned at an enormous mahogany desk, typing page after glorious page, a trash basket at her side filled with sheets of smudged paper and crumpled mistakes. Sometimes she was a young woman who looked remarkably like Francie, other times she was a sour old snort of a woman with a cat who liked to wander precariously along the window sill. Sometimes I would seat myself in her richly upholstered swivel chair, making the same blunders and errors, but also making up strange and complicated worlds for people to walk around in. It seemed odd to me that I had conflated the book's author with its main character. If anyone had asked me before my revelation, I might have said *A Tree Grows in Brooklyn* was written by Francie Nolan. Betty Smith, I said out loud, naming my hero to myself, making her as real to me now as Francie had been.

It was my great luck to have a mother who played the piano and left good books strewn around the house. I remember sitting next to her on the piano bench, watching her fingers move like trapped birds across the keys, my spine erect, my ribs trembling like the smallest branches on a tree, the notes rising upward into the air. She read books with titles like *War and Peace* and *Let Us Now Praise Famous Men,* the poetry of Robert Frost and e.e. cummings. Later, when she went to nursing school, she brought home biology, chemistry, and psychology textbooks. These books were my education, but they were also my friends. They informed me there were other, larger worlds outside my door.

Even though I read *A Tree Grows in Brooklyn* around the same time that I began writing poems, I never thought of it as an influence on my writing life. After all, it was a novel. But looking back, I can see how the brief bit of prose that forms the prologue to the book has helped to shape my poetic sensibilities.

> There's a tree that grows in Brooklyn. Some people call it
> The Tree of Heaven. No matter where its seed falls, it makes
> a tree which struggles to reach the sky. It grows in boarded-
> up lots and out of neglected rubbish heaps. It grows up out of
> cellar gratings. It is the only tree that grows out of cement. It
> grows lushly . . . survives without sun, water, and seemingly
> without earth. It would be considered beautiful except that
> there are too many of it.

My project as a woman writer has been to write about women, to bring to light those who are invisible in their ordinariness. Models for my own writing became poets Sharon Olds and Carolyn Forché. Olds gave me permission to write passionately about domestic life, and Forché offered me the beauty of language and image as well as the power of a controlled voice. Both are women of my own generation who see the universal in the particular, heroism in the ordinary, and who are involved in the project of recording the emotional history of the world. Both are witnesses to the ordinary life. Both are woman artists.

My mother is an artist, a musician, though she would never call herself this; she never performs publicly and rarely composes music. "I simply play the piano," she tells me. "I don't do it for any reason beyond love." As a child, I saw the daily devotion she brought to her craft, the passion and discipline with which she approached it, the years of sacrifice she made toward the achievement of an ideal. The tired housewife, registered nurse, and mother of six, who walked to her piano and sat down, was not the same woman who rose an hour later and turned to face us in the living room. In that hour we had been transported, and she had been transformed; she was no longer our mother, but a woman made of music. For the rest of the day, I studied her hands as they gripped the wicker laundry basket, threaded a needle, emerged dripping from a sink of gray dishwater, or held firm my bruised knee, gently swabbing it with a puff of cotton dipped in iodine. It was mysterious to watch her extraordinary hands, chapped, blue-veined, the delicate fingers long and expressive, capably perform with precision and grace so many ordinary tasks. I can see how it is her hands that have given me the encouragement and permission to become an artist, the courage to be a poet. I also see how my poetry is an attempt to recreate, in language, the subtle rhythms and fierce crescendos of my childhood, to enter the world with an ear toward its complex harmonics and jazzy discords. And so it is appropriate that my book, *What We Carry,* is dedicated to my mother, and that "The Ebony Chickering" is the centerpiece of a project that seeks to acknowledge and pay homage to the extraordinary lives of women.

A few years ago, I found a used copy of *A Tree Grows in Brooklyn* in paperback. I bought it because, unlike my old copy with the green, fake-leather cover, the spine broken and exposed, the individual threads woven in and out of the yellow pulp, it contained an "author's note." This is what Betty Smith wrote in 1947:

> I remember how once as a child I read a book which appealed to me deeply and I wrote my heart out in a letter to the famous author. He never answered. I was hurt and ashamed that my heart had been rejected. I vowed then to try to write a better book than he when I grew up and to answer any letters I got about it. So I answer each letter if only to say: 'Thanks!' Sometimes it gets to be a chore and I want to give it up but then I worry that I may hurt someone the way this long-ago author did me. So I keep on answering the letters.

I never wrote to Smith. I wouldn't have thought one could do such a thing. Even after my discovery that she was a real person, I couldn't quite believe she existed. What I know now is that she dwells in me to this day, standing alongside my own mother, another artist who gave me permission to write, to succeed, and to fail on my own. And they stand beside my aunt, who has painted in oils and watercolors since I was a child, who would never call herself an artist and yet continues to paint, giving her work away as gifts to family and friends. And she stands next to my third-grade teacher, who trilled her R's and my eleventh grade drama teacher, who reminded me to enunciate clearly, and my summer coach, Bonnie, who taught me how to throw and catch a ball, and my college teachers in philosophy, history, science, and literature. All women. All extraordinary. All artists.

I could say Betty Smith taught me how to read, to hear a story, to care so much about words on a page that they began to form the shape of a living being who took up residence in my heart, and in doing so, taught me how to write. I could say it was the mysterious nature of expression, that the words themselves were the source, the music of them, the secret enchantment of words appearing in my mind and then coming to life in my hands. I could say it was my mother's hands. Anything I say about how I became a poet will obscure some element of the whole, leaving something or someone out. I'm not sure what or who first admonished me to write, but I know this: I am grateful to have been invited into the world of language, and into the world of women, and allowed to watch them work. To have been shown, at an early age, what capable and magical creatures they are. □

THE SHADOW
OF THE BIG MADRONE

Philip Levine

My first night in California I spent in a motel in Squaw Valley; it was late summer of 1957, and the place was being developed for the coming winter Olympics, but in August it was all but deserted. I was alone, having left my wife and two sons in Boulder with my mother-in-law while I came ahead to find a place to live. I'd come down with some sort of flu the day before and had stopped just before sunset west of Salt Lake City. I'd been seeing things on the road all day, things that weren't there, flying cats and dark birds who disappeared in the shadows; these creatures were beginning to spook me, but it wasn't until I'd stopped for an ice cream cone that I realized I hadn't eaten all day and had no appetite. Very strange. The guy who made the cone for me said the usual, "Hot enough for you?" and as I nodded it struck me that I wasn't sweating at all, but everyone else at the roadside stand seemed stricken by the heat. My forehead was burning, so I drove on to the first motel and stopped. All I had with me were a few aspirins and some antihistamine pills, which I took. Before dark I was asleep. When I wakened some hours later. I was so drenched with sweat I had to move to the other bed. At 5 A.M. I wakened again and got on the road ahead of the truckers and crossed the Great Salt Flats before the day's heat came on. At a filling station in eastern Nevada I asked the man at the pumps what the speed limit was. I watched his eyes behind his sunglasses move across the hood of my teal-green '54 Ford two-door. "I don't think you got to worry," he said. Before dark I'd climbed my third mountain range in as many days. Never before had I seen such dramatic landscapes. In Michigan anything taller than a Cadillac is considered a hill.

Taking a small radio into my Squaw Valley motel room I still felt light-headed and slightly high on nothing. I didn't know if it were due to the altitude or the previous day's fever. I lay out on one of the beds and listened to the most amazing radio program I'd ever heard, on a station called KPFA in Berkeley, which was hours west of me. The program consisted of one man with an extraordinarily affected and ponderous professorial voice reminiscing on the famous people he'd known personally. His articularity and the range of his associations dazzled me: Gertrude Stein, Jung, Robinson Jeffers, Isaac Bashevis Singer, Tu Fu. When the program ended, I discovered it had been Kenneth Rexroth. A true poet on the radio! What a rich world I'd stumbled into. I was so excited I had trouble sleeping that night and once again rose and dressed in the dark. By noon I'd crossed the Bay Bridge into San Francisco singing "I Cover the Waterfront" in my glorious baritone that fortunately no one heard. Ahead of schedule, I stopped at a diner for coffee and directions and was amazed by the graciousness of the counterman, who drew me a map all the way to Los Altos on the peninsula south of the city. There I would find the home of Yvor Winters, who had generously offered to put me up until I found a place to live.

That spring I'd received a short terse letter from Winters informing me that he'd chosen me to receive a Stanford Writing Fellowship. This was a great relief for my wife and me; our second son had come down with a childhood form of asthma and we were advised to seek a more gentle climate than that offered by the Midwest. For two years I'd been teaching technical writing in the Engineering College at the University of Iowa as well as one course each semester in Greek and Biblical literature, and my first teaching had left me with very little time for my own writing. It was the first job I'd had in years that left my hands clean, and I'd begun to wonder if I could both live on my wits and write my poetry, for I'd written much more while I was doing unskilled work in Detroit.

Winters' home on Portola Road was surrounded by a high redwood fence. A brief notice on the gate warned that there were dangerous dogs within; one was advised to use caution and enter at risk. I advanced gingerly. The door was answered by a tall, spare woman whom I'd interrupted at household chores; I took her to be the maid. When I explained who I was and why I'd come, she gave me a wonderfully open and welcoming smile and asked me to be seated. In contrast to her strong, dark features her voice was faint and barely audible, her hair drawn back and largely hidden under a flowered scarf. I recalled a little magical poem by Winters' wife, the poet and novelist Janet Lewis, which depicted the slow movements of a cleaning woman, and I wondered if, like "some Elsie" of William Carlos Williams' famous poem, she were the same maid grown to womanhood.

> Girl Help
> Janet Lewis
>
> Mild and slow and young,
> She moves about the room,
> And stirs the summer dust
> With her wide broom.
>
> In the warm, lofted air,
> Soft lips together pressed,
> Soft wispy hair
> She stops to rest
>
> And stops to breathe,
> Amid the summer hum,
> The great white lilac bloom
> Scented with days to come.

Seated, waiting for the arrival of my mentor-to-be, I finally figured out that the woman had told me he was not home. As the time passed slowly I could only hope he would not be too long in returning. I noticed a photo of Winters on a bookshelf behind the television set. (Did Yvor Winters actually watch television?) He had aged considerably since the famous photo of the severe young poet I'd seen in various anthologies; it presented a grim bespectacled fellow in shirt, tie, and leather jacket who seemed in the throes of some terrifying moral problem. This man was actually smiling, perhaps caught off guard, and the woman who stood at his side in the photo was this very housekeeper, who I realized must be Janet Lewis.

The older man I soon met rarely smiled, but for reasons I cannot explain I felt even on that first Friday afternoon that there were stores of affection in him that went unexpressed. He arrived in, of all things, a tiny red English sports car, and directing his gaze steadily into my eyes introduced himself; before I could take my seat again he explained that the chair I'd been using was his and he directed me to another alongside it, and thus we sat side by side conducting one of the most awkward conversations I'd ever been a part of, but Winters was very good at silence. Minutes passed while he stoked and puffed on his pipe; occasionally he would issue forth a heavy sigh. He seemed not in the least curious about me. I noticed that every few minutes he stared into a mirror that gave him a view of the front door to the house, which was behind him and to his left. Apparently he had never heard Satchel Paige's dictum, "Don't look back, something might be gaining on you," or if he had he'd discounted it. Much to my surprise at five that afternoon Winters turned on the TV set to watch a rerun of a Robin Hood serial. "Pay close attention," he said, "it may improve your accent." So he was not entirely without a sense of humor.

That very night I learned he was a devotee of prize fighting. He later assured me that prize fighters and poets had one central thing in common: pride in their abilities. A fighter who doesn't think he can beat everyone in the world is no good to anyone, he told me once, and a decent poet has the same confidence. I too was a boxing fan, and this brought us together at least once a week to watch the Friday night fights, on which we usually bet when there was a difference of opinion. In my incredibly short career as a boxer I'd learned considerably more about the art than Winters had. I had quit after my marvelous coach, Nate Colman, had advised me in one pithy sentence regarding my chief strength. "Your ability to take a punch," Nate had said, after watching me get whacked about by a mediocre light-heavy, "is worthless if that's all you're doing." Would that most literary criticism went so directly to the point. I never lost a bet to Winters, though the largest I ever won was a quarter. I wouldn't say he was not a gambling man, for he'd taken an enormous gamble on his talent as both critic and poet.

Like many Californians of that era, Winters was a hater of some actual or imagined Eastern fight establishment that had managed to keep deserving West Coast fighters permanently from glory. He especially hated Floyd Patterson and his manager Cus D'Amato, neither of whom was part of any fight establishment; they had refused to give the new California hope, Eddie Machen, a shot at the heavyweight title. (When Machen finally got his big chance, he was knocked out in the first round by Ingemar Johansson, and thus it was the Swede who was given the opportunity to dethrone Patterson.) I soon came to realize that Winters felt about prize fighting exactly as he did about poetry: both were rigged by some all-powerful and invisible Eastern conspiracy, and he and his favorites would have to wait on the outside pending some miracle. For all I knew then, he was correct on both counts.

One thing was sure: he knew a lot more about poetry than he did about prize fighting. I later learned that he'd come to boxing as a young man living in what he called "the coal camps" of New Mexico, where he had gone to live on doctor's orders to combat a case of TB he'd come down with in his early twenties in his native Chicago. In order to support himself he'd taught high school in New Mexico, and it was there he'd had to learn the fine art of boxing so as to enforce discipline in his unruly students. It was impossible for me to guess what Winters had looked like as a young man; at 57, when I first met him, he had a thick sturdy body, one that in no way resembled that of the classic fighter. His shoulders were narrow, his beam broad, his arms short, and only the thickness of his neck suggested a fighting past. On Saturday nights, he told me one afternoon as we waited for the fights to come on TV, there had been public fights on the streets of his town in New Mexico; anyone and everyone was welcome to participate, and for weeks he had hoped to take part. But even then he was no fool: not being a large man nor one carrying the heavy muscles of a miner, he needed to learn the finer points of the boxer's craft, and they had been taught to him by an old ex-pro. Laying his pipe aside, he stood in his slippered feet, and showed me how his coach schooled him in the use of both right hand and left hand. He then faced an imaginary foe and pumped both hands forward and back like someone aping the movements of a cross-country skier. "Like this!" he exclaimed.

"I never lost a fight."

"You were lucky," I said.

"After the first fight I had no more trouble from those big miners' sons in my classes."

"You were lucky," I repeated.

What did I mean by that, he wanted to know. I explained that the stance he'd taken was the worst possible one to assume if you were serious about not getting hurt. "Really," he said, "how should I stand?"

I'd known him some months when this exchange took place, and never before had I gotten his attention with such intensity.

"Show me what I'm doing wrong," he said. I began a modified imitation of the first lesson my old coach had given me; modified because Nate always concluded that lesson with a little passage he entitled "Who's boss," in which he'd pin back the ears of the fledgling by delivering a variety of punches that showed the student how little he knew. I had no confidence in what might happen if I were to manhandle Winters, so I merely demonstrated to him that he could neither move backwards nor forwards with any speed and that if I were to shove him he would land on the seat of his pants. I took the proper stance and demonstrated in slow motion that while I could easily reach him with my left hand, he was more than a foot short of me and his entire body was open to my punching whereas most of mine was distant and guarded. He nodded slowly taking it all in. I then arranged him in my stance, left arm and left leg forward, and then showed him how easily he could move forward or back, right leg following left forward, left following right backwards. "That's the way Joe Louis always moved forwards," I said. Winters asked how he moved back. "He never needed to move back."

"That was a counterpunch," Winters said and smiled. He was enjoying this, so I went on to explain that Ray Robinson didn't always follow those basics because he was so gifted he could improvise, he could square up or cross his legs or punch off one foot because he could get away with anything. Winters watched as I demonstrated these moves. "Louis looked like a natural," I said, "but he was someone who mastered the basics so well they looked natural. A Sugar Ray or a Wallace Stevens comes along once in a century." Winters was taking it all in, his cheeks flushed, his mouth loose and relaxed, his eyes wide. He asked me how I'd learned all this, and I told him about my great coach, who had once been the amateur middleweight champion of the U.S. and was in training for the Olympics when World War II put them on hold for twelve years. "He was a lot like you, Mr. Winters," I said. (Yvor Winters, whose first name was actually Arthur, never encouraged me to call him anything except Mr. Winters, and I was comfortable with that name.) "Nate was a purist," I went on, "he believed in the art of boxing and at the same time he thought it was ugly to punch another person for money, so he rejected professional boxing and instead spent his evenings giving free lessons to kids like me." Once again we were seated, and I went on to describe encounters in the gym in which Nate had easily bested professionals, on one occasion a middleweight contender who'd given Graziano a tough fight. Nate had him down in less than a round; he did it all with body punches.

"Body punches?" Winters said.

"Yeah, they were wear light bag gloves; it was a real fight. The guy wanted to hurt Nate, he wanted to take the mastery of the gym away from him. Nate couldn't let him do that, so they went at it with the bag gloves, and Nate didn't want to break a hand on this guy's big hard head, so he destroyed him on the body." On previous occasions Winters had narrated some of the great West Coast matches, and I had merely listened. Now it was my turn to discover what an intense listener Winters could be. What I spoke of I'd actually seen, whereas the fights Winters related were part of a general mythology that passed from one man to another, few of whom had witnessed the events. When I'd finished, Winters nodded. "You must be one hell of a fighter yourself."

"No," I said, "I stunk."

"You're being modest."

"No, I'm serious. my balance is mediocre and my hands aren't nearly quick enough. I fought light-heavies with quicker hands than mine. I'm strong and durable, and that may make it in poetry, but it's no good in fighting."

Winters nodded, convinced.

On the first Saturday night in Winters' house I was invited to a party he and Janet were throwing. The guests would include his former students Wesley and Helen Pinkerton Trimpi, as well as the historian H. Stuart Hughes, who had left Stanford to head the history department at Harvard. Trimpi was also just back from Harvard, where he'd gotten his doctorate. Winters stated flatly that Trimpi was now the finest Ben Jonson scholar alive and his soon-to-be-published work would prove it. The old man was pleased with this turn of events; he thought Wesley would be a finer scholar than a poet. Helen was the true poet. He'd seen almost nothing by her in years and so had no idea if she'd realized her potential. I reminded him that in one of his poems he'd urged the young poet to "write little" and do it well. Of course, he said, but he hadn't meant *that* little. I asked him why he'd ever suggested the notion of writing little; why hadn't he urged the young poet to write a great deal and write well? "You're being facetious," he said. I insisted I was serious. Didn't every artist practice his art as much as possible so as to develop his abilities? He turned his head away from me and muttered, "You're not being serious."

Stuart Hughes, the grandson of Charles Evans Hughes, was one of the funniest looking men I'd ever met; he had a long horse jaw, enormous teeth, and his eyes seemed set at different latitudes. He was a wonderful talker, utterly winning and charming. His wife was a dark beauty in the Jackie Kennedy mold though lusher. The two of them moved with an ease and grace that only made Winters seem like more of the plodding bear than he was. Trimpi turned out to be a very tall, elegant young man with perfect manners. His wife was plain but handsome in an interesting way. I noticed her large, strong hands and her resemblance to the West Virginia hill women I'd worked with in Detroit and guessed her origins were far from her husband's. I immediately liked her.

Within a few minutes Winters began to bait both men. Hughes had deserted Stanford for Harvard. Trimpi had returned in triumph with his fine Eastern degree, and the old man pretended to be pleased with neither. The full force of his attack did not come until Hughes made his splendid announcement: His gorgeous wife was pregnant with their first. "You're happy about that?" Winters said.

"We're utterly delighted," said Hughes, a man in early middle age about to become a father.

"You're making a mistake," said Winters. Janet tried to shush him, but he turned to her and stated baldly that the man was old enough to hear the truth.

"And what might that be?" asked Hughes.

"Having children is the most difficult and thankless task in the world."

"Arthur," Janet said, "you know you're exaggerating."

Arthur insisted he was not. He had grown flushed and angry and would not be stilled. Hughes shook his head back and forth and comforted his wife with small pats on the back. The room had stilled. Suddenly he turned toward me where I sat on a bench in the corner hoping to remain invisible. "Mr. Levine," he said, "I believe

Janet mentioned you had two sons who would soon be arriving."

"Yes," I said.

"Would you say that being a father is as dismal as Arthur had stated?"

"It has problems," I said. "It can be very tough when your kids get sick." I did not look at Winters.

"All of you, wait until they grow up. Then you'll know what I'm talking about." Winters said.

The next morning all seemed forgotten, and Winters offered to make breakfast for me. I declined and helped myself to coffee and a bowl of dry cereal, while he slowly downed a bowl of chili, odd fare, he admitted, for breakfast, but he claimed his pipe smoking had all but killed his sense of taste and he needed something potent to rouse him each morning.

I was very comfortable in the Winters' bungalow, an old, stuccoed, unpretentious house that he'd added rooms to as his needs grew with the coming of children. The large back yard was dense with fruit trees Winters had planted, and at the very back against the tall fence stood the kennels for what remained of his famous line of show dogs, which once included a grand champion. Now there were only three aging Airedales who barked and leaped in a frenzy every time they caught sight of a stranger. Next to the garage was a large, unshaded area which Winters had transformed into a vegetable garden and where he worked several hours most summer mornings.

On this Sunday I decided to look up an old Detroit friend, the poet B. A. Uronovitz, who for some years had been a protégé of Rexroth's. I'd lost Bernie's address and so phoned Rexroth, who was listed in the phone book. The woman who answered gave me the address. Overhearing me call, Winters remarked that I should not tell any of these people where I was staying, for they might do me harm. I told him that the man I was going to see was a very old friend. "I'm serious," he said. "Don't mention my name. Any friend of mine is their enemy." Later that day I located Bernie; when he asked me where I was staying I told him. "Winters," he said, "he's an old friend of Rexroth's, who thinks he's a great poet."

When I returned late that evening from San Francisco, I was still excited by the city. Aside from New York I'd found it the most attractive American city, and when I told Winters he told me I'd been taken in. It was not what it seemed. I believe the truth was Winters disliked cities, and in spite of his enormous intellectual curiosity he had seen very few of them. He'd spent much of his growing up in Chicago and Los Angeles, and now he found them both "dangerous" — Chicago because of the violence of its population, Los Angeles because nature could easily erupt in sudden outbursts of floods and earthquakes. He hoped never to see either again. "I hate to sound nostalgic," he said, "but all of this" — and he turned his palms up in an uncharacteristic gesture — "all this 'development' has ruined this valley. When I first came here, it was the most beautiful place in the world, a glorious garden. There was no traffic. You could hear the coyotes yipping at night." I asked him if they weren't a threat to his dogs. "A threat to Airedales? You don't know much about dogs. The Airedale can manage anything its size and most things larger."

One of Winters' favorite games was to take me out into his yard and quiz me on the identity of his trees, especially the fruit trees. On my second afternoon in Los Altos he'd introduced me patiently to such exotic species as apricot, fig, almond, plum, olive, lemon, loquat, and orange. Thereafter every few weeks he would conduct an oral exam, which to his delight I would invariably flunk. Now and then I'd get one right, and he would nod solemnly to show his approval. Once I suggested we take a walk down the nearest large boulevard, El Camino Real, and we'd see how many automobiles he could identify. "Mr. Winters," I said. "I'm from Detroit. I didn't see a tree until I was in my late teens." He asked if that were true, and I explained it was meant as a joke.

He did not have a great sense of humor, and yet he found very unfunny things funny. For example, his description of Chaplin's *City Lights* (the sole movie he recalled seeing) and Kafka's "Metamorphosis" were the same: he called each "mildly amusing . . ."

I often missed his tone completely, especially during that first week. He owned a little female cat he indulged but was not fond of. The cat's mother had been a great favorite, but a year before she'd gotten out of the compound and had been run over. Telling me this he groaned and said in a voice that recalled W. C. Fields, "All along I assumed she would be the pet of my old age." I thought he was doing a parody of the fanatical cat lover I expected him to despise, but when I laughed he turned towards me with anger and shouted, "I'm serious, boy, this is no laughing matter!"

That same day he decided it was time to find out how closely I could read a poem. He asked me to fetch a book from his living room shelf, opened it to a particular poem, and, handing it back, commanded me to read. The poem was the beautiful "Lullaby" by Gascoigne.

"I know it," I said.

"Read it again. It might edify you."

Written in the sixteenth century by the poet George Gascoigne, the poem had been a favorite of my Iowa friend Don Petersen, who I thought misread it exactly where Winters was most interested in it. It is a simple, repetitive lyric in what Winters called "the plain style," an unadorned style he admired above all others. In it the speaker sings all his various faculties to rest as he prepares to die. The poem was first published in the early 1570s shortly before Gascoigne's death at thirty-five. It begins:

> Sing lullaby, as women do,
> Wherewith they bring their babes to rest,
> And lullaby can I sing too,
> As womanly as can the best.
> With lullaby they still the child,
> And if I be not much beguiled,
> Full many wanton babes have I,
> Which must be stilled with lullaby.

And so he devotes a stanza to his youthful years, another to his gazing eyes, his wanton will, his "loving boy" addressed as his "little Robin," and in the final stanza summarizes his farewells:

> Thus lullaby my youth, mine eyes,
> My will, my ware, and all that was,
> I can no more delays devise,
> But welcome pain, let pleasure pass:
> With lullaby now take your leave,
> With lullaby your dreams deceive,
> And when you rise with waking eye,
> Remember then this lullaby.

I reread the poem certain I knew what the question would be, but it came in a form I hadn't expected. Winters wanted to know why, when he included the poem in *The Oxford Book of English Poetry*, Quiller-Couch had omitted the penultimate stanza.

"I suppose because of the reference to 'little Robin,'" I said. "He was a late Victorian, and it was a popular anthology."

"What does 'My little Robin' refer to?" he asked.

"His prick," I said.

Winters was silent for a long moment. I though he might be displeased that I'd passed his first test so easily. "What he calls 'my ware' in the final stanza," I added.

"Don't be vulgar," he said, in a quiet voice, "the word is penis."

Winters turned our attention to matters of prosody. He had me read to myself Googe's little poem "On Money," which begins "Give money me, take friendship whoso list," and argues for the greater constancy of money over friendship. Winters had a curious affection for the poem although he seemed largely unconcerned with money. We haggled in a friendly way over the scansion of the line, "Believe me well, they are not to be found," which he heard as perfectly regular and which to my ear contained a substitution which allowed it to echo speech. He asked if I'd read his latest piece on prosody, which he expected to be his final word on the subject. It had appeared in a recently published collection, *The Function of Criticism*, which I didn't own. That night when I retired I found a fresh, clothbound copy of the book on my bed inscribed to me by Winters. The next morning when I tried to thank him he brushed my words away.

In Iowa we had been living poorly but surviving on my teaching, which paid $3,600 the second year. I'd been informed by my boss in technical writing that for an outstanding first year's service I was getting a $100 raise. But our rent in Iowa City had been $60 a month. Palo Alto and the surrounding communities were another world. I spent a depressing hour at the Stanford student housing office going through files only to discover that not a single listing was within our reach. One house that came complete with pool, gardener, and four-car garage, went for $900 a month and would have devoured three fellowships the size of the one I was getting. In East Palo Alto near the Southern Pacific tracks I found a second-floor apartment, unfurnished, that went for $120 a month. Janet Winters came with me to make sure it was a reasonable deal. For a moment we both stalled on the fact I wouldn't be able to get in until the first of September, which was two weeks in the future. My wife and kids were flying out in a few days. Janet urged me to take it anyway, assuring me that she would work something out. "You don't have room for all of us," I said. She had something else in mind.

That night we went to dinner at the home of one of Janet's dearest friends, Marie Louise Koenig, who had once taught chemistry at Stanford. It was a curious evening, for both Winters and Marie Louise were terribly shy people in company and especially in each other's company. It fell to Janet and me to create whatever conversation there was. The place itself was astounding: a wild little island of several acres in the heart of neatly trimmed Los Altos Hills. The wide front porch gave on to an enormous lawn that sloped down to a thicket of young trees, weeds, underbrush, and unpruned shrubs. The area behind the house was even less tended, for Marie Louise hadn't gotten to it as yet. Wild as it all seemed, Janet assured me it was highly cultivated compared to what it had been only a few months before. To the west of the two-story mansion was a large open area covered with gravel; it was dominated by an enormous oak tree under which stood two picnic tables. It was here we sat out to have drinks before dinner.

Winters asked if I would like a highball, an expression I had never heard outside of the movies. I declined the offer. He asked if I had something against drinking. I explained that I just wasn't drinking anything stronger than wine. "Good thing," he said, "there's too much drinking in our profession." I asked which one he meant, teaching or writing. "I was thinking of teaching," he said, "but there's way too much in the other as well." It didn't stop him from having a highball, which Marie Louise brought.

It was late enough in the year that the shadows began to lengthen and darken even before we went in to dinner. In the fading light Marie Louise broke through her shyness and apropos of nothing recited the ending of a poem by Winters.

> There is no wisdom here; seek not for it!
> This is the shadow of the vast madrone.

She got the last line wrong and said "big madrone," but Winters did not correct her; he only sucked on his unlighted pipe, blushed, and nodded cordially. I thought I saw a bat circling near a side entrance to the house. Janet seemed to be watching it also, but she said nothing. Marie Louise turned her light blue eyes on me and said in her thickly accented English, "Does that not say it exactly, Mr. Levine, just exactly?" I agreed. She went on. "I say those lines over and over to myself out loud every day at this time. 'This is the shadow of the big madrone.' Isn't that just perfect?" There was something so genuine and infectious about her enthusiasm that I nodded in violent agreement, though in truth I had no idea what she was talking about.

The next morning Janet informed me that she and Marie Louise had worked it out. My family would spend the ten days in the mansion. Marie Louise had a separate basement apartment She'd been thinking of renting it out, and this was an opportunity to see if it were suitable. I felt odd about accepting such generosity, but Janet assured me I'd be doing Marie Louise a favor. She had recently been abandoned by her husband, a physicist who was now in the Stanford administration; he had dumped her for a graduate student, a woman in her twenties. Since then she had been through some very rough times, but she seemed to be coming out of her depression. Janet felt that what she needed most was something to distract her, some outlet for her enormous energy. She had hoped the house would provide that, but one elderly woman in so vast a place had not answered the problem. Perhaps one elderly woman and a family of four would.

Amazingly, it worked. Marie Louise and Fran hit it off in no time, and within a day of our installation we were on a first-name basis. My two sons, Mark and John, loved her huge estate with all its overgrown nooks, its buried gazebos and duckless duck ponds. The second day John managed to fall into one of them and create a minor tragedy. Most evenings I was assigned the task of grilling a huge slab of meat outdoors. Within a few days Marie Louise's handsome second son, George, began to come around with his girl friend, Paulette. The two of them were studying architecture at Stanford and were planning a trip to Arizona to meet their master, Frank Lloyd Wright. George was in training for the coming summer Olympics and bicycled for hours every day up and down the nearby hills. He seldom mentioned his older brother, Fred, though it was obvious that Marie Louise was proud of his record in law school and his position as editor of a prestigious Eastern law review. I gathered he was more conservative and plodding by nature than George, who Winters had told me except for the muscles and tan was a ringer for their father, who was never mentioned.

Thus I was the senior male, the only father in this odd salad, and as such I was accorded the role of wise one and raconteur. Marie Louise and George urged me each evening to recite from the book of my past, to tell old family tales or describe the characters I'd met while growing up and working in Detroit. It never occurred to me that this could be a source of interest to anyone. They seemed especially entranced by the tales of Zaydee, my tiny Russian-Jewish grandfather, who at just over five feet had been a dominant character in my life. One evening while grilling a huge steak and drinking red wine with George I told of how even in my twenties Zaydee could startle me with his moxie. We were on our way home from work in my older brother's convertible Chrysler, of which he was inordinately proud. Zaydee was in the back with his house companion, Lemon. (My grandmother had walked out on Zaydee after forty years of marriage, claiming she couldn't take another day with that man.) The old man recalled that during World War I he had hawked peaches and sweet corn on this very street. My older brother was skeptical until from the back seat came an ear-shattering cry: "Ripe freestone peaches, dollah a bushel!" The whole street had jerked to attention. "How did it sound?" asked George. But before I could do my imitation, George called his mother, and I began the tale over again for her delight.

When Marie Louise laughed, she did so with all of herself. The sound would erupt in great barks from her sturdy upper body. She was a short woman and appeared even shorter than she was in her sack-like cotton dresses that fell almost to the ground, but she was very powerful. I learned this on my second day in her house when she asked me to help her move a stone bench. The thing weighed well over two hundred pounds and I was reduced to stumbling after her and gasping for breath as she directed us effortlessly. With a single exception, the only time I ever saw her grant herself the luxury of tears was when she laughed. Her fine eyes would crinkle at the corners, and she would let go in a great flood, which she wiped away with the back of one hand while the other held her abdomen as though she were capable of shaking apart. When she'd catch her breath she would ask me to stop, but as soon as I did she would ply me with wine and urge me into talk. She was, I think, the only person who enjoyed these long evenings more than I. Once George and Paulette departed and Fran went off to put the kids to bed, Marie Louise and I would do the dishes, though at first she was wary of allowing me into the kitchen. It was then we would have our most serious conversations on such themes as the young (which somehow did not include me), on poetry, on fiction, on history, on America, and, after some evenings had passed, on the subject of Germany. "I cannot go back," she would say. "I cannot."

Born into an upper-class family in Saxony during the first decade of this century, in her teens she had decided on a career in the sciences. It was while doing her university work that she met the young physicist who would become her husband. Those were the glory days of physics, and the two of them had met such notables as Heisenberg, Dirac, and Oppenheimer. Married, they moved to Leiden; Marie Louise began graduate study in chemistry, and her husband embarked on his teaching career. It was clear that Europe was drifting toward war; when a teaching offer came from America, her husband accepted it. Her hands immersed in the milky dishwater, Marie Louise would shake her head back and forth and half-shout, "No, I cannot, I cannot go back!" From memory she would describe the Saxon landscape she yearned for, the small neat farms with their startlingly green fields trimmed right down to the roadsides, the narrow roads themselves which she walked or rode on her bicycle, the thick stands of oak and fir left to suggest the great forests this civilization had been cut from. "It was not like here in summer," she would repeat. "Here it is burned to brown or yellow, here is no rain from June to October, but there it was a green world." She'd give me a little smile. "Yes, I came to womanhood in a green world. It makes a difference. But I cannot go back."

The apartment on Emerson Street, named for one of Winters' least favorite writers—which I took to be a good omen—had to be furnished. Janet sent out the word, and within no time we were picking up an assortment of abused chairs and hideous lamps from her friends. Marie Louise offered a decent couch from the downstairs apartment, to be returned before we departed, and within a few days several trunks and cartons full of bedding, towels, and kitchen equipment arrived from Iowa by rail. We purchased some inexpensive beds, and Fran set about making curtains. We were in business. Seeing the apartment, Marie Louise declared we needed several chairs she could locate to go around the dining room table, which was also absent. She insisted on calling the tiny space off the kitchen a dining room. She crinkled up her eyes and walked to a particular spot and announced, "The dining room table will go here."

"Where will it come from?" I asked.

"Philip, you will make it."

When I told her I was no good with my hands, She brushed off my reservations. "With my help you. will make it." I would also make, with her help, a coffee table. "You are entering the bourgeoisie, Philip, and today it is impossible to arrive without a coffee table." Back at her place, hidden away in a large storage room in the basement, she showed me two unfinished pieces of wood. One was a slab of oak about four inches thick and curiously warped; it was a long slender rectangle that vaguely suggested a coffee table. She thought for a moment and then said black was a fashionable color, black would hide the scars, and it so happened that she had a can of black paint she had no use for as well as brushes. "Legs?" I asked. No problem. She knew where we could purchase short iron legs for next to nothing. The other piece was more attractive but presented greater problems: a six-foot square of plywood that was unfinished at the edges.

"We will locate thin pieces of lath and make it perfect. And the grain is very good. I have all the tools we require. Go home and dress in your worst clothes and then come back." She looked me over carefully and laughed. "Those clothes will do." And so we went off to a hardware store, which turned out to be "her" store, and bought lath, sandpaper, stain, and lacquer to finish the "dining room table." On her own she purchased wood putty which she presented to me back at her house. "With this you will cover the few mistakes you make. Anyone who can write a poem that can please Arthur can become one of the world's great carpenters. Don't you think?"

Calling on the skills I'd developed in my eighth-grade shop class, I worked alone for hours in her dim basement. Once things were assembled and ready, she insisted the painting and staining go on outside behind the house so I would not asphyxiate myself. Meantime she was working down the hill from the front of the house using a chain saw to remove the underbrush that hid those trees she'd decided were her favorites. Every few hours she would appear with two beers in hand, and we would take a break.

"I do not mean to pry, but I cannot help noticing that you sing when you do this work. I do not think," she went on, "that when you work on your poetry you can sing. I think you actually prefer this kind of work."

I told her that I'd largely done manual labor and I felt comfortable with it. "Yes," she said, "I recognized that immediately in you. I think we have this in common. Inside each of us is a peasant waiting to be allowed to live a simple, decent life, but the intellectual keeps the peasant working at all hours behind a desk. I don't know why we accept this." She smiled, her eyes reduced to mere slits in the light that filtered through the trees. Late afternoon in early September, and already an autumnal crispness was in the air. She took my empty beer bottle, and we rose to go back to our work. "Philip," she said, "this is great."

At the first meeting of Yvor Winters' graduate writing class there were three students. One was the other fellow chosen by Winters; he was an attractive young man named Francis Fike who I had learned was an ordained minister, though he lacked a congregation to minister to. The third was a young poet from Philadelphia who had come to Stanford on a Woodrow Wilson Fellowship. It struck me that without fellowships Winters would have no students at all. Winters had told the third poet to bring a selection of his poems so that the professor could decide if he should be admitted to the class. In Winters' place I would have grabbed at any warm body, but it was immediately clear he felt otherwise. We three students sat in silence while the old man, his face closed in a determined scowl, read slowly through the sheaf of poems. After some minutes of this Winters looked up and said, "This line doesn't make any sense."

The young poet, a short, dark-haired, neatly dressed fellow in slacks and sweater, seemed far less distressed than I would have been. "What line is that?" he said.

Winters read in his deep sonorous voice, "'At dawn the young grass wakens on darkened legs.' The movement wouldn't be terrible if it were in the proper context of blank verse. As it is it's set in a passage that's not verse at all and it doesn't mean a thing."

"It is poetry," the young man said, "and it has a meaning."

Winters leaned back in his leather swivel chair behind the great oak desk. He was within easy reach of his poetry library which was arranged alphabetically in bookshelves that reached to the ceiling on three of the walls. The three of us sat on metal chairs across the desk from him. It was a small, cozy room with a single window that opened directly on to the quad. It was easy to see why Winters spent so much time here. "Perhaps there are three lines of verse in this one, three of . . ." and he scanned the page ". . . three out of twenty-five or so, but this line means nothing." The young man began to answer, but Winters held up a palm. "I've lived with grass. I've grown every kind of grass you can possibly think of, even Jimson weed, and I can assure you the line means nothing."

The young man repeated himself. "It's poetry, and it has a meaning."

"If it's poetry," Winters said, puffing on his pipe and shrugging his shoulders, "it's very bad poetry, but in any case it has no meaning."

The young man sat calmly and in silence. He appeared to be totally above the fray, confident in his abilities as a poet and in no way distressed by Winters' display of candor or bad manners. I thought to myself that if every class went this way I was in for one tortured year. I hoped I was just seeing Winters' version of what Nate Coleman had called his "who's boss" initial lesson. A few minutes passed. Outside I could see the students passing quietly down the bricked paths of the quad. Everyone seemed to behave as though they were in a library. I'd had no idea the name Stanford resonated so potently. Winters broke the silence. "You insist it has a meaning. Fair enough. Tell me what it is."

The young fellow rose from his chair, nodded first at Fike, then at me, and at last addressed Winters in a quiet, unruffled voice, reaching first across the desk to take the sheaf of poems from Winters' hand. "It means, Professor Winters, that I'm dropping this class." He padded to the door without looking back and was gone from our class forever. Perhaps feeling that some explanation was due Fike and me, Winters told us the young chap was a recent graduate of the University of Pennsylvania, all honors student with a brilliant record, but his intelligence had been wasted there for no one on the staff of the English department of the

University of Pennsylvania had even the vaguest idea what a poem was.

Winters went on to explain that we would meet here once a week on Tuesday afternoons and each of us would bring at least one poem to class. In the meantime we were expected to attend his course in the English lyric poem which met two early afternoons a week, though we weren't obliged to register for it. If we wanted the credits, he would certainly accept us as students. There was no text for this class save our own poems, but several anthologies of poetry were required for the other course, and we would be expected to read the relevant chapters of his own collections of criticism, *In Defense of Reason* and *The Function of Criticism*. We were dismissed.

Out in the quad I learned that Fike had taken the incident with the young poet from Philadelphia more to heart than I. For one thing they were about the same age, for another he felt Winters' attitude toward him was similar. The old man had told him that he'd chosen him for the fellowship only because "all the other applicants were worse." (I could only hope I wasn't one of the "worse" poets.) When I asked him what he'd thought of the Philadelphia poet, he smiled and said, "Gutsy guy."

Winters' class in the lyric poem was something else. It was conducted in a large airy room whose windows opened on the quad. The teacher sat at the darker end of a long wooden seminar table at which all of the registered students also sat. They numbered fewer than twenty. There were four regular auditors who sat in chairs against the wall; it was a rare meeting that did not bring one or two visitors. Winters always dressed formally. His tastes leaned toward gunmetal gray suits, white shirts, and muted ties, the sort of outfit one expected on an Allstate claims adjuster circa 1957. The graduate students, who made up about half the class, also tended toward formality in dress; many were teaching fellows, and this was Stanford.

The assumptions he made concerning who was in attendance were curious. For example, during the first meeting of the class he remarked that the students would be disappointed if they expected to hear the sort of truths they'd gotten from reading the criticism of T. S. Eliot and John Crowe Ransom. All the students knew that Eliot was the most celebrated poet of the era, but I would guess that none of the graduates had read his criticism. Ransom was better known then than now, but he was hardly a name to conjure with. From Ransom he segued into a diatribe against the prose of Allen Tate and R. P. Blackmur, which he declared was unintelligible. He slammed his fist down on the heavy wooden table and announced that criticism was not meant to replace poetry or prose fiction; its functions were to elucidate and evaluate, and the second function was the first in importance. No one in the class had said otherwise. "I know what you're thinking," he said, "you've come from classes in which these men are regarded as the great minds of the age, and what you're hearing now is heresy." My guess was the students were wondering what the hell they were in doing in his course.

He then passed out mimeographed sheets containing three poems: a sonnet by Shakespeare, a Renaissance poem entitled "Fine Knacks for Ladies," and the Googe poem "On Money." He asked the students to rate them, but only to themselves. He then read them aloud in his monumental style. Whenever he read poetry, he pitched his voice at its lowest and chanted in a monotone, always coming to a heavy pause at the end of the line. His reading style was meant to underline the differences between speech and poetry, and nothing about it was meant to entertain. Poetry was a great source of moral suasion; forget that and you missed the whole point. It's possible the class did miss the whole point, for his voice and reading style so dominated the language itself that the poems sounded much alike. To my surprise he preferred the sonnet and liked least the Googe poem. "Fine Knacks for Ladies" he found delicate and lovely, a fine poem of its kind. He declared Shakespeare's rhythmic mastery far beyond the other two poets', and the poem was serious. I would later discover he could hear poetry as acutely as anyone I would ever encounter, though he did not always prefer what sounded best. How else explain his preference for Fulke Greville to Ben Jonson? When the class ended I had an inkling of how much I could learn from this man.

On the top floor of the Stanford library I found a spacious, well-lighted room that housed the university's rare book collection. Most afternoons I used it I was the sole customer. Here I located for the first time *The Collected Poems of Elizabeth Daryush* in four beautifully printed volumes. Daryush was the English poet who wrote the first truly successful poems in syllabics, a form she and her father had developed to escape what he, Robert Bridges, had called the "tyranny of the iamb." It was Winters, of course, who had put me on to these poems, and ironically at Stanford it was Winters who made the iamb's rule so tyrannical as to be called Tsarist. Winters also directed me to certain new poems by Thom Gunn in syllabics, but I felt such a powerful sympathy for these poems that I was afraid to study them for fear of falling under their spell. Most of the Daryush poems were genteel and sweet; they had very little to do with any life I knew, but they moved with such grace and poise that I fell in love with their artistry. My favorite was "Still Life":

> Through the open French window the warm sun
> lights up the polished breakfast-table, laid
> round a bowl of crimson roses, for one—
> a service of Worchester porcelain, arrayed
> near it a melon, peaches, figs, small hot
> rolls in a napkin, fairy rack of toast,
> butter in ice, high silver coffee-pot,
> and, heaped on a salver, the morning's post.
> She comes over the lawn, the young heiress,
> from her early walk in her garden-wood,
> feeling that life's a table set to bless
> her delicate desires with all that's good,
> that even the unopened future lies
> like a love-letter, full of sweet surprise.

"Still Life" was also Winters' favorite, for he had no more love for the "aristocracy" than I.

The woman who ruled over these books was firm in her refusal to allow me to withdraw them for even an hour from the room. I explained to her that I was at Stanford on a fellowship to write poetry, and I wanted the inspiration these poems could give me. She nodded perfunctorily. A tall, slender woman in her mid-thirties, in her flowered silk dress she seemed dressed for the role of tea-pourer at an English lawn party. She looked as though she were a lot closer to the world of Elizabeth Daryush than I was. She was sorry, truly, but the books did not circulate. In fact, she wished there was a requirement that readers wear white gloves when they handled them. Not knowing what condition my hands were in, I considered hiding them, but finally thrust them out. She laughed. She hadn't meant anything personal. If I were a Stanford graduate student, she was sure my hands were clean at all times. I asked if that were a metaphor, and she gave me a blank look. "Do you have pencil and paper?" she asked. I had paper and pen. She was afraid a pen would not do. She gave me a #2 pencil and pointed out a sharpener on the wall. The books could not be handled by anyone using a pen, for they might be permanently defiled. Then she took me through the exquisite nature of the binding, the paper, the print itself. These were precious books indeed, and I was welcome to copy in pencil any poem I wanted. For this I purchased a mechanical pencil called an Eversharp that promised to copy forever, and when the next day I showed it to the trustress of books she smiled at my ingenuity.

Life was proving easier in California than it had been in Iowa. I was not teaching courses I had no enthusiasm for, the weather was mild, Mark's school was two blocks away, and our son John was not plagued by the childhood form of asthma that put him in the hospital several times the winter before. But by early November it was clear we lacked the money to get us through the Christmas break and to the second check from Stanford. I applied for a temporary job with the postal service and was immediately taken on for a minimum of six weeks. Assigned to a mail route in a quiet neighborhood in Palo Alto, I thought at first I was incredibly lucky until the roving dogs got wind of me. One Sunday I told George, Paulette, and Marie Louise how Winters had given me a sure-fire method of dealing with dogs: fill a squirt-gun with ammonia. One shot on the snout would do the job.

Marie Louise found the story very revealing. Winters, the man who raised show dogs and claimed to love them more than people for their breeding and courage, had discovered what he called a "sure-fire" method of dealing with his favorites. Dark clouds were scudding over the trees. The sun had dropped from sight, and the air was turning cold. It had rained much of the morning, and now it looked like it might rain again. "That man is all contradictions," Marie Louise said. We had had a very early dinner and were now gathered around the Franklin stove in Marie Louise's favorite room, a porch that had been glassed in and turned into a sort of rumpus room. She had been in a very festive mood, especially when the rain let up and we were able to grill. "Do you know German poetry, Philip?" she asked.

"Don't get started on that," George said.

She ignored him. "Do you know any German poetry?" she asked again.

My mind seemed to go blank for a moment. Finally I recalled that as an undergraduate I had helped a language major translate some simple lyrics by Heine.

"But you don't know German," she said.

A friend had asked me to help her translate the poems for class. She would recite them over and over and translate each word and phrase, and together we would settle on something that seemed to catch the original. I remembered being pleased with what we'd gotten. "What were they about, the poems?" asked Marie Louise. There were only three; two had been love poems, the nicest one was about a pine tree. Marie Louise began to recite in German. *"Ein Fichtenbaum steht einsam/Im Norden auf kahler Höh . . ."* and then she translated haltingly, "A fir tree left alone stands/In the far northern country in the terrible winds . . . " She stopped. "I cannot do it right," she said, "I have no talent for this. But you already know the poems." She worried a thumb across her forehead, and turned from the stove to face me. "So you think we Germans can write poetry?"

"It doesn't matter what I think. Of course gifted Germans write poetry."

"Why? Why are you so sure?" she demanded.

"For centuries they have given us great painting and perhaps the greatest music in the world, so why shouldn't they be able to write poetry?" The room was growing dark. Marie Louise had turned back to the stove; she stood ramrod stiff stuffing in small branches. After she stripped the leaves, she crushed them to a powder which drifted to the floor. "German is an old and great language. . . ." Finally I recalled my own reading. "Even in the versions I read, Rilke's *Duino Elegies* and his sonnets were remarkable. And the songs of Brecht . . ."

Marie Louise recited the little lyric by Heine, ending with the phrase, *Auf brennender Felsenwand*. She repeated the last phrase. "It starts in the far north, but it ends in the burning sands. Such a little poem, but it covers the whole earth. We learn these poems when we are very young, and they are always with us."

"Yes, we have poems like that. Fran can recite dozens of little poems her mother taught her." I had learned no poems as a child, but I didn't mention that.

"Once I tried to recite this little poem of the fir tree to Winters. Do you know what he did?" She had seated herself on a little stool across from me. She smoothed out her long skirt. Before I could answer, she went on. "He held up a hand like a traffic policeman, just like a policeman, and told me to stop. He did not want to hear it." Why? I asked. "Because Germans are sentimental. They can praise the beauties of fir trees and clouds and then murder millions of people. Philip, what do you think? Is he right?" George tried to interrupt, but she shushed him.

I didn't know how to answer. I suddenly didn't even know how I felt. I knew only that I wanted to say something that would be of comfort to this woman. "I don't think those who did the killing were those who wrote the poems."

"You don't know German poetry," she said, "how can you be sure?"

"Because it's obvious," I said, knowing at this point nothing was obvious except that this woman was a lifegiver. Outside the rain had started again. George switched on the porch lights, and we could see huge drops pelting off the hood of my car. He raced out the front door and clattered down the stairs. We could see him gathering up the heavy sweaters he and Paulette had left near the grill. In a moment he was back, laughing, his fine blond hair streaming with water.

My wife even then was a far more social creature than I. She wanted to invite Arthur and Janet to dinner as a thanks for their many kindnesses toward us. I tried to dissuade her, but she is also far more stubborn than I. One Friday night after the fights I asked if they would be available. Winters nodded and said they would if I would provide a decent wine and enough of it. What was enough. "Two bottles should do us. You and Janet barely drink," he said laughing. I confessed I didn't know a decent wine from STP. "When you know what your wife is preparing—I can only hope she is preparing the meal and not you—give me a call, and I'll tell you the names of some decent wines. And where to get them." We had chicken tetrazzini and a Charles Krug Grey Riesling that sold for $1.35 at the time.

Winters arrived in a fury. No one had told him we lived on

the second floor; he'd had trouble negotiating the outside metal stairs. "They're dangerous," he said, puffing. I was sure he was angered because even such a short climb revealed how pitifully out of shape he was. A highball calmed him down. The boys had been fed and were next door watching television with our neighbors. We sat to break bread. Winters ate slowly and methodically, trying his best to taste each mouthful. Janet praised the meal and Italian cooking in general.

The four of us were seated comfortably around the table Marie Louise and I had constructed; things were going better than I could have hoped for. Winters decided that I would be the proper arbiter in a small quarrel he and Janet had had. A look of dismay passed across Janet's face. "I'd say it was only a disagreement," she said. She knew what was coming.

Winters put the matter to me so formally and so precisely I had no doubt he'd rehearsed his words in his mind. Just the day before Janet had been composing a scene in a new novel she was working on. In this scene two boys of fourteen and twelve, brothers, wrestle playfully on a large bed, their parents' bed. The play has a serious aspect, for the boys know that one day they will be rivals in important matters. "Janet," he said, "used the word *roughhousing* to describe their play. I'd like to know what you think of the word."

I stopped eating and took a sip of wine. I could only put this off so long. Winters had put down his knife and fork. Janet and Fran went on eating. I thought the word was all wrong; for one thing it seemed terribly dated to me, but then Janet was twice my age. Finally I said I found the term too genteel.

"Genteel!" Winters exploded. "It's not genteel. It's far too coarse. I can't stand the word. It's simply too coarse." Janet was trying not to laugh behind her napkin, but she wasn't doing a very good job. Arthur turned to her. "You will ruin the entire scene with that one word."

Now it was Janet whose curiosity was aroused. She had stopped laughing, but it was clear she was still enjoying herself. She wanted to know if there was a word or an expression I might employ that would convey her meaning and not strike me as too genteel. She would rather be slightly coarse than genteel, but she was not up on the words young boys might use today. I considered the terms boys might actually use and immediately rejected them.

One explosion from Winters was enough. "I think I would use the expression 'horsing around'," I said, knowing perfectly well I would not use it. Janet seemed less than thrilled. She would think about it. Winters had gone back to his tetrazzini with a vengeance.

Encouragement came from an unexpected place. I had sent my friend Henri Coulette two of my syllabic poems, "Small Game" and "Night Thoughts over a Sick Child," and Coulette wrote back from Iowa City that not only he but several other poets as well were excited by them. Even Don Justice was fascinated by their movement. They were probably the first original poems I'd written. When I'd switched from traditional meters to syllabics, something seemed to have been released, and without any preamble I was writing in my own voice. Coulette was anxious to learn from me how I'd managed to handle this form so quickly and with so much confidence. The truth was I had no idea. I had painstakingly copied all of the syllabic poems of Elizabeth Daryush, and then I made some tentative stabs at a few poems of my own in the form, and one day I was writing with this new authority.

"Small Game" was the first one I showed to Winters. He studied it at great length in silence. At last he looked up and said, "The rhymes are very good. The syllabic movement is fine, very fine. A poem in syllabics is seldom very good, but the details here are wonderfully observed." He paused for a puff at the unlighted pipe and said, "What is it about?"

I was caught off guard and, looking down at my own copy of the poem, improvised. "It's about the man who speaks in the poem and the life he leads and the relationship of that odd life to whoever might read the poem."

Winters humphed. "You could probably say that about dozens of poems. I'm not sure you've said anything." I thought the poem was so clear it needed no explanation. I didn't dare quote the MacLeish line about poems simply being.

Before Winters handed the poem back, he asked me to repeat my explanation, and I fumbled through it again. He nodded. When the quarter ended, he sent me a one-page report on my progress. Again he stated that the rhymes and movement were very good, the details well observed, but he could no longer figure out what the poem was about. He recalled that when I'd explained it he had half-understood me, but he no longer recalled what I'd said. He added that I might better use my new-gained skill with syllabics to write poems that were about something. I am still unsure what Winters meant by "about something." The poem was about something the way poems are about something, though it did not employ the language of abstract thought that was so dear to him. It would be too easy to say he despised the particulars of our lives and thus the language that presented them. I knew that was untrue. I had seen the man in his garden and walked with him through the dappled light that fell from his trees too many times to doubt his pride in what grew and his love for growing things. He did not feel awkward and unlovable when he bowed to his strawberries and his tomatoes; he did not feel in any way threatened when he yanked tenderly on a branch of his favorite olive tree and spoke of the pleasure its fruit, properly cured, had given him. Calm and peaceful as it was on an afternoon in Los Altos, this was not Eden Garden; it was in the here and now, and Winters fought the grower's common pests—the snails, the aphids, and tomato bugs— and mostly he won. Perhaps "the mid-day air was swarming/With the metaphysical changes that occur," but the dust that rose was that of common earth worked by a man. At their best his own poems testify to what he often did not, that "the greatest poverty is not to live/In a physical world."

Even then I understood his distrust of poems in syllabics. The writing often comes in a great rush, it finds the rhymes quickly, and the poems take their own course. Winters had written a great deal of free verse, some of it gorgeous, but he had disowned the best of it and in some cases even reworked the same material in ponderous couplets. He believed in the morality of form, in the struggle of reason to discover what the imagination had gone in search of. In syllabics and even more in free verse the intuitions seize the poem and direct it, and Winters was frankly distrustful if not fearful of the intuitions. More than once he'd insisted that it was through his abiding trust in his intuitions that Hart Crane had come to his sad and watery end. It could not, he repeated, have ended any other way. According to Winters, all who wrote poetry flirted with madness and self-destruction: the more powerful the imagination the greater the danger. To survive one practiced a heroic vigilance. All the days I knew him he lived that vigilance.

That year Winters gave his first public reading in many years.

It was held in the auditorium of the San Francisco Museum of Modern Art, and the proceeds went to the NAACP. (Much to the surprise of many of his readers and in sharp contrast to his clones today, Winters was a liberal as well as an ardent believer in equality, racial and otherwise.) A few nights before the reading he phoned and asked if I would help with his preparation. He asked me to make a list of those poems I thought essential to a final presentation. My list was modest: "To the Holy Spirit," "At the San Francisco Airport," "On a View of Pasadena from the Hills," "Sir Gawaine and the Green Knight," and "By the Road to the Airbase." I'd written the names out on a piece of paper which I handed to him. "Is that the whole list?" he said, "I'm not going to be able to fill an hour with these."

"Of course not," I said, "This is just a core of what I believe you must read." I realized I'd goofed again. "I'd like to hear you read the Theseus poems and Marie Louise's favorite, 'Manzanita.'" And then I recalled "The Journey," much of which I liked enormously. I suggested that for the sake of variety he might read the free verse version.

"What free verse version?" he asked, looking at me in alarm.

I explained that in an anthology in the Stanford library, a book with a title like *The American Caravan*, I'd found an early free verse sequence which included passages that he'd reworked into "The Journey." He slapped his forehead. "You found that in our library. How did you locate it?" There'd been no trick to locating it, for it was listed in the card catalogue under his name. "My God," he said, "I thought all that was dead and buried. I wrote that over thirty years ago. It was the best I could do at the time. I shouldn't still be hounded by it." I said truthfully that I thought it was wonderful free verse, though I did not add that it was clearly written under the influence of Williams. "Yes, I knew what I was doing, which is more than I can say for most poets writing free verse."

When Winters went off to fix himself a drink, I looked at the little *Collected Poems* published in the early fifties by Alan Swallow. Fewer than one hundred and fifty pages with notes, it is an ugly duckling of a book. It seemed perfect for Winters. All the words were there and in the proper order, and the binding is sturdy enough to keep things together for a lifetime. When he returned, Winters asked me to listen to a reading of the Theseus poems, a long, brilliant sequence full of gore and sex which traces the life of the Athenian hero from his youthful slaughter of virgins to his exile in old age and his final betrayal. Winters read mainly in his familiar monotone, though now and then the power of the blank verse would seize him and his voice would ride out on a dazzling riff. As he read I asked myself, Who is he talking about if not himself. I knew the poem was written before he was forty, and yet it read like a preparation for the end, the finale. What *chutzpah*, I thought. He'd even outdone Tennyson with his aged Ulysses. When he'd finished, he sat in silence for some time. "No," he said, "I can't read it."

"You've got to read it. It sounds marvellous." It had, and I couldn't believe he didn't know it. "It's superb blank verse and like nothing else." I wasn't flattering him, and he knew it.

"I couldn't read it before all those people." He went through "To the Holy Spirit," which he read in so quiet a voice that I had to bend to listen. Finally he read the little poem that closes the book, "To the Moon," whom he addresses as the "Goddess of poetry." The poem, written before he was fifty, ends,

> What brings me here? Old age.
> Here is the written page.
> What is your pleasure now?

Much to the shock of his students, even in class he could not resist discussing his impending death. "That's all," he said, "I'm losing my voice." Then before I could rise to leave, he added, "It's not much, is it?"

"I thought you read very well," I said.

"I don't mean that. I'll read well enough. I mean this little book of poems." He held it in his open palm and shook his head. "I don't think it's enough, I don't think it will last. The criticism is a solid achievement, but this is too slight. I can barely fill an hour with poetry. What do you think?" He was asking me!

"They are true poems," I said, "they will last." He shrugged and looked unconvinced.

There were curious omissions in his preparation for criticism and inconsistencies in his views. Nothing stopped him from generalizing about the greatest novels ever written, though he never mentioned the Russians, Germans, or Asians. One late Friday afternoon before the fights came on, Janet and I were talking about one of her great loves, the historical novel, a form which she was the master of. I happened to mention my favorite, *War and Peace*. "Is it really as good as they say?" she asked. I told her I thought it was the greatest novel I'd ever read. I turned to Arthur to get his opinion only to learn he'd never read it. Had he given up after *Anna*? No, he had read nothing by Tolstoy? And Dostoyevsky? He'd tried *The Notes of an Underground Man* and found them mildly amusing. Chekhov? No, he didn't know Russian, and he didn't feel it was worth his time to bother with translations. He read the French, the Spanish, and the Portuguese in the original.

Janet said, "Do you think I'm missing something?"

"I think you're missing the greatest fiction ever written, but don't take my word for it," I said. "Read anything by Chekhov."

Arthur was skeptical. He hadn't the slightest doubt the work was highly overrated. Besides there wasn't time now to learn Russian, and even if there were he had better things to do with his time.

On another occasion I discovered he had a highly selective memory. I had mentioned meeting John Crowe Ransom on two occasions and finding him a very cordial man. "You were duped," said Winters. "I know he has that reputation, but that's not Ransom." He went on to describe this curious animosity Ransom had toward him; Winters found it suggested mental instability on the part of the Kenyon critic. I remarked that if I'd been called a savage in print by Winters I might harbor some animosity toward him. "I never called him a savage," he said quite firmly. I wasn't sure quite how he'd put it. I leafed through the pages of *In Defense of Reason* until I located the passage, which I read aloud:

> Ransom's devout cultivation of sensibility leads
> him at times to curiously insensitive remarks. In comparing
> the subject of a poem by Stevens with that of a poem by Tate,
> he writes:
> The deaths of little boys are more exciting than the sea
> surfaces—a remark which seems worthy of a perfumed elderly
> cannibal.

I never wrote that," he said. I handed him the book, and he read the passage from the beginning to its brilliant conclusion. Then he burst out laughing. "Well," he said, "maybe that explains it."

I found it comforting to learn that Winters had views he never put into print that made it clear he had a wider range of appreciation than the later criticism would suggest. Once in class he scolded both Fike and me for the poems we'd shown him for the past several meetings. "I hate to sound romantic," he said, "but there simply isn't enough feeling in what you've been writing. These are interesting ideas and nothing more." On another occasion he chided me for lacking imagination. When I asked him since when that had become so important, he made it clear it was central to poetry. I was miffed by his remark, which was accurate, and so I countered that he was sounding like Coleridge. "Fine" he said, "I'm in good company."

Perhaps the most interesting revelation concerned Yeats. In order to comprehend Winters' preference of the work of T. Sturge Moore to that of Yeats, I'd been reading the two side by side. I confessed to Winters I'd found Moore small beer by comparison. He admitted that Moore had his limits. What had I been reading by Yeats? I named several of my favorites, "Lapis Lazuli," "Dialogue of Soul and Self," "The Tower," and remarked that I found enormous authority in the writing. "Of course you do," said Winters, "he was the greatest stylist of the century." He took in my stunned response. "I'm not deaf, boy, I can hear how marvelous the writing is. I hate what it's doing." His duty was not to be seduced by the enemy.

Some subjects were off limits. On several occasions I tried to get him to talk about Hart Crane, but I managed only once. Their single meeting was in Los Angeles during a Christmas break at Stanford. Winters had gone south to visit his parents in Eagle Rock, and he and Crane had arranged a meeting. He told me it hadn't gone well because Crane had been in bad shape. I thought by "bad shape" Winters meant he'd been out of his mind, but Winters corrected me. Crane had been or claimed to have been in a bar fight and was seriously bruised and cut about the face. As far as Winters could tell, all Crane wanted to do was drink and get in another fight. I asked him what he thought of Crane's appearance. He'd expected a slender, aesthetic-looking man, and instead he'd faced a thug. "Crane had the thick arms and shoulders of a professional boxer," he said. "There was something brutal even in the way he moved." I got the sense he'd felt intimidated by Crane.

Physical strength and its lack were very important to him. He loved to tell a story he'd gotten from J. V. Cunningham. Cunningham had told him of the enormous physical power of Robert Lowell, and to illustrate it he'd described an episode in a hotel room during which it took two strong men to subdue Lowell. The struggle had lasted five minutes. Winters wanted to know who the men were. When Winters found out they had been Cunningham and Allen Tate, he'd roared out his laughter. Tate and Cunningham couldn't subdue Janet.

As the winter quarter neared its end, we were once again running out of money. Out of the blue I got a call from my brother in Detroit. He wondered if I would like to work for him purchasing bearings the government was offering for sale. He sent me long lists of what he was interested in, and I went to the Oakland Navy Yard and the huge military warehouses at Benicia. I would phone him about the accuracy of the lists and the condition of the bearings, and then enter his bid. If he got the stuff, it would be my job to pack and ship it to Detroit.

I'm not sure why I hated the work so much. Each day seemed to begin well enough, usually with a spectacular drive across the Bay Bridge where whatever fog enshrouded San Francisco lifted and the sunlight sparkled off "the chained bay waters." The drive to Benicia was lovely. I'd cross a huge old metal drawbridge north of Berkeley, turn east, and then drive through verdant hills to descend into an isolated valley with a view of an inlet of the great bay of San Francisco. From miles off I could see a huge mothball fleet of battleships, cruisers, destroyers, and even two aircraft carriers, that had survived WWII. On the road to the warehouses I would pass acres of obsolete tanks, armored personnel carriers, and neat rows of a hundred and fifty-five millimeter howitzers that looked like toys. Everything was painted a dull olive.

If I checked in at the office early enough, I would find my military contact present and sober. My brother advised me to be as inconspicuous as possible and to linger long past noon, for by lunch time even the enlisted men would abandon all pretense of working, and I could look at whatever material I wanted, even that labeled off-limits. The bearings were sold by lot numbers, and each lot was displayed on a separate skid. With no one watching it was easy enough to exchange a carton from one skid to another, to trade desirable bearings for undesirable ones. Of course if I were free to do this, so was anyone else. I was sure my brother would be cheated. I also felt that some of the men who worked there were waiting to be bribed to look the other way or protect a purchase. My brother moved among such men with a bravado and confidence that entirely escaped me.

If he got the bid, I would wait hours for a truck to arrive, usually one with an exotic name, an Iroquois or a Mohawk. An enlisted man would fork-lift the skid out to a loading dock, and then he and the driver would watch and smoke as I toted the cartons into the truck. If a box were unusually heavy or bulky, one of the men might suspend his sports talk to give me a hand. I'd sign the bill of lading, fail to bribe the driver to insure a safe voyage, and as the early darkness began to fall head back across the valley toward the old steel bridge to Richmond and the deepening waters of the bay. Even a job badly done has its rewards. The ride back was even more delicious than the ride there, and by the time I got home all I could recall were the lovely hours from noon until three when the great warehouses were empty except for me and the softened California light, sifted down from the high ceilings, turned golden in the dust. Somewhere off in the distance I'd heard music, perhaps a radio or the songs the wind makes through raftered lofts.

The highlights of the spring quarter were visits by the famous. I cannot now recall what Kenneth Burke spoke on for an hour or less to a dozen graduate students in a seminar room in the library. He had a strong profile and beautiful white hair about which he seemed to have no vanity. There was no one there to introduce him, so he introduced himself, rising from the couch on which he was seated alongside a handsome, elderly woman. I can remember that he began by remarking that he couldn't recall if the academic hour began like the psychiatric hour at ten after the hour. His relaxed and droll manner seemed out of place at Stanford as did the sturdy corduroy jacket he wore, the sport shirt, and the felt carpet slippers at which the graduate students tried not to stare.

Frank O'Connor came next; his reading was widely heralded and drew an audience of several hundred. To celebrate the event Wallace Stegner invited the entire faculty and student body of the graduate writing program to a party at his house on Page Mill

Road, which at that time was an undeveloped prairie southwest of the campus. That evening, much to our surprise, Winters was there downing a highball when we arrived.

I was seated on a chair across from Winters when O'Connor introduced himself, and then asked was this Professor Winters not the very Professor Winters who preferred the work of T. Sturge Moore to that of Yeats. Winters said he was indeed the man. O'Connor, swaying above him with a drink in hand, burst into laughter. Not seeing the trap being laid for him, Winters added, "And I did it for good reasons."

"And what might they be?" said O'Connor.

"The obvious," said Winters, "he was a far better poet and a more serious man."

"Moore a serious man!" said O'Connor, almost choking on his drink. "Can't for the life of me imagine what's so serious about straining to become the last Romantic poet of the nineteeth century, especially during the twentieth century."

"There's nothing Romantic about Moore's mature poetry," said Winters.

"Perhaps you're right," said O'Connor, "you're the expert," and then he quoted the last lines of "Silence," a favorite of Winters':

> Give me dry eyes whose gaze but looks intense!
> The dimpled lobes of unreceptive ears!
> A statue not a heart! Silence so kind,
> It answers love with beauty cleansed of mind.

O'Connor went on. "Perhaps romantic is not the right word, perhaps the word is adolescent. I could accept such from a great boy-poet like Keats, but in a man of our years, Professor Winters, it's unseemly."

"Keats was not a great boy-poet," Winters mumbled, gnashing down on the stem of his pipe. O'Connor wanted to know if America presently boasted any poets superior to Keats, boys or otherwise, and Winters gave him the names of the two greatest living poets writing in English, J. V. Cunningham and Edgar Bowers. O'Connor frowned. Sad to say, he'd failed to keep up with American poetry. These names were unfamiliar to him. "They wouldn't by any chance be former students or cronies of yours?" he asked.

Winters glowered and then pointed to me. "He can tell you who they are."

I was speechless just long enough for O'Connor to lean down and whisper in my ear, "Show some cheek, lad, and tell the old man to stuff them." O'Connor then raised himself to his considerable height, staggered, and announced to Winters and all those present that he suddenly knew exactly who Winters reminded him of, to a T. Winters did not take the bait, so O'Connor went on. "You are the identical twin of Dylan Thomas. Did you ever meet him?"

"Ridiculous," said Winters. He probably loathed Thomas as a person and a poet above all his contemporaries. "Thank God, I never met him."

"You would have loved him," said O'Connor. "You're exactly like Dylan. The only thing he ever loved was poetry. In no time you'd have been drunk in one anothers' arms reciting poetry. Take my word for it."

Flushed and trembling, Winters rose from his chair and called out, "Janet, we're going, we're going right now."

For several thousand dollars Robert Frost spent part of an April afternoon on our campus. It so happened that our writing workshop met earlier the same day, and just as Fike, Winters, and I had begun our debate on why someone ought or ought not to pay two dollars to hear Frost, the good gray poet—now gone white—passed by the window of Winters' office. Winters himself whitened. Frost peered in, and the room went utterly silent. "My God," said Winters. Frost turned, and then we heard his slow steps as he continued down the walkway. Winters breathed a sigh of relief "I never dreamed he'd seek me out," he said.

"You think he's looking for you?" Fike asked.

"Who else?" said Winters. "He'd like to get even for what I wrote about him."

"It wasn't that bad," I said.

"It was that bad, and he's read it," said Winters. "I know his reputation for wisdom, but he's a mean and spiteful man. He'd like to hurt me." When Winters had asked me what I thought of the essay, I told him I'd been surprised by it, for he hadn't chosen a single line of one of Frost's better poems to discuss. "I wasn't trying to make him look good," said Winters.

Halfway through the Frost reading I was thinking that Winters was entirely wrong about the character of the man, for he appeared so at ease and comfortable with a huge audience he had enthralled. In the middle of a recitation of "Mending Walls," he burst out at someone in the audience, "Sit up! Where were you raised?" All twelve hundred of us unslumped. He then went back to the poem, faltered, and claimed the poem had been ruined for him. When the reading ended, the audience rose in silence and filed slowly out. None of us liked being hollered at.

In December, a job at Los Angeles State for the following year had looked probable, but when the Soviets launched Sputnik, priorities changed, and the two sections of poetry writing I'd been offered were transformed into sections of technical writing. I decided to look elsewhere. Sacramento State interviewed me. Sequestered with their dean of humanities and his sidekick, the chair of English, in a windowless room in the Stanford Placement Office, I watched the dean give the chair the high sign. Then came the sixty-four dollar question: "What would you do as advisor to the literary magazine if the editors showed you an obscene story they wanted to publish?" I answered with the wrong question: "Did the story have any literary merit?"

Two days later it was Fresno State. Their dean was a wiry guy with a face unfurrowed by thought. This will go badly, I said to myself. He handed me a catalogue that described all the courses offered by the English department and asked which I could and couldn't teach. I was not up to *The History of the English Language* or *Beowulf*. Much as I loved his work, I wasn't the right person to teach Chaucer's poetry. I realized this was not going well. You never got a job in Detroit by saying you could not do something; if need be, you could draw the perfect circle or load boxcars on boxcars. I amended my remarks. In a pinch I could teach Chaucer, and Shakespeare would be a delight. (I'd even read the plays.) Everything since then was right up my alley, though my specialty was Creative Writing. Amazingly, they were looking for someone to teach fiction and poetry writing.

The dean seemed delighted to have discovered a true Renaissance man, willing and able to teach almost the entire gamut of courses, so he began to sell me on Fresno before Yale or Princeton discovered I was available. Located smack-dab in the middle of the San Joaquin Valley, you could reach the Sierras in less than an hour, the Pacific in less than two. You could have the best of both worlds. It was unexcelled for hiking, which was his favorite sport. Horse racing was my favorite sport, but I made no mention of it, nor did I mention that hiking was what we did in Detroit when the car broke down.

Winters was elated when a week later the chairman of the English department invited me down for an interview. Two of his former students were now teaching at Fresno State, and he gave me a letter of introduction to present to the older, a great favorite of his. I would see beautiful country, he told me with delight, unspoiled by development, California as it once was. I would cross the Pacheco Pass, named for the legendary Mexican bandit of the last century. Carefully he drew me a map and marked the various sights I should be on the watch for. Early the next Monday morning, I headed south on 101, turned east at Gilroy, and headed for the pass. I drove beside miles of low brown fields of onions and garlic; the Ford filled with delicious perfumes. As I climbed, the hillsides burst with delicate white flowers called mouse tails. The rains had been heavy that spring, and soon the fields were thick with lupine, wild mustard, and poppies. Cresting the pass I saw my first magpie flash the underside of its wings. A few miles later my first Joshua tree, ancient and gnarled. Is this what it looks like east of Jerusalem? I wondered. I stopped for gas in Los Banos where I picked up a hitchhiker, a little skinny guy who lived south of Fresno. "What you wanna go there for?" he asked, "City full of cotton pickers." On 152 we passed Berenda Slough; the fields were so flooded the water lapped at the center line of the highway. After Chowchilla I turned south on 99 toward Madera. The names were music. Winters was right; I would have to learn Spanish. My passenger asked me to drop him off at Klein's Mammoth Truck and Car Stop; I did and went on alone to find the campus. Luckily, I got the job.

My school days were coming to an end. I was thirty now, and I'd had all of the student life I could take. That summer I taught poetry writing through the malls and made my last visits to the Oakland Navy Yards and Benicia. Several nights a week Marie Louise Koenig invited us over, and we began spending much of our weekends there. Janet Lewis, Winters' wife, would frequently appear. George and Paulette, Marie Louise's son and his girlfriend, had gone off to meet their idol, Wright, at Tallesin West, and come back stunned and slightly disappointed. George had been reminded of Winters, for Wright was another "great man" who knew everything and tolerated no sass.

Sitting out under the oak tree one Saturday night after dinner, Marie Louise Koenig told me the story of Winters' reception of the Bollingen Award. A telegram had come, Janet had told her, and when Arthur returned from teaching she waited while he opened it. Winters read in silence and then handed the telegram to Janet with the remark, "Too little and too late." Janet wanted to go east for the award ceremony, but Arthur claimed he was too old to be travelling across country by train. He'd done it once and hated it. "Is that typical of the man?" said Marie Louise.

I said it was and it wasn't. Sometimes he was totally self-absorbed and grim, and at other times he could be as generous as anyone I'd known. "Arthur generous?" she said, disbelieving. I told her how for hours he had taken me line by line through difficult French poetry, the great work of the past hundred years, Baudelaire, Rimbaud, Corbière, Valéry. Once he discovered I was serious in my interest, there was no limit to the time he would spend. It was past 8 P.M., the sky was still a clear blue. She poured me some red wine and asked if Janet knew of this generosity. "I must tell her," Marie Louise said, "she will be so pleased. I think she seldom sees this side of him, though I thought many times if I asked him for help he would be there. I think he is reliable, yes?"

I agreed. I was sure he wanted to be generous, but often he simply didn't know how. He was a very clumsy man. She agreed. He was clumsy in every way. "I do not know how Janet has put up with him all these years," she said. "I prefer to be alone. Do you think he is ever happy?"

"He should be. He has everything he could hope to have."

"What do you mean?" she said. "He would say he has nothing."

"He's done his writing. It's there," I said. "The criticism is original and eccentric, but it's brilliant and it's what he wanted to establish. All over the country younger poets and critics are competing for his attention."

"I'll bet he treats them like his children," she said. "I'll bet he constantly shows them his dissatisfaction."

Winters had complained to me that his son had gone into ballet dancing. He'd urged him to give it up; as far as the old man was concerned the boy was an "underpaid athlete."

Marie Louise started gathering the dessert dishes. "Yes," she said, "I know people whose sons are in jail, and they are happy they will be out soon." She laughed outrageously, holding her belly with one hand. "That is the sort of humor I have learned from you Philip. Oh," and she dried her eyes, "tell me, have you ever seen him truly enjoy anything?"

"Yes, when he was reading those French poems to me. There were times I thought he was transported. He's the most serious lover of poetry I've ever met. Much of his pleasure was pure generosity; it came from seeing my pleasure in discovering this poetry. He already knew it all." The work Winters had done was enormous. He'd learned a Breton dialect in order to understand Corbière. One afternoon he'd spent two hours going through a particular poem so that I might follow it. I told Marie Louise that Winters had sketched out the history of a particular Christian festival the poem dealt with.

Marie Louise sat back down. "Arthur knew church history? He doesn't even believe in God."

"He believes in poetry," I said. "You can't begin to understand the poem unless you know about Saint Anne and the Pardons." I'd never heard of her, but once Winters filled me in all the pieces of the poem came together. It ends with a stunning description of a wandering rhapsodist, an ancient crone, who for a few coins will recite your favorite tale of misery. As best I could I quoted from memory the conclusion of the poem: "If you ever see her in her old army clothes it will be a holy day. Remember, she's our sister, so give her a pinch of tobacco and you'll get back her ugly smile and a true sign of the cross." Winters loved the passage; he went over it again and again to make sure I got it. I told Marie Louise that he'd been so moved I thought he might cry, but he didn't.

In the falling darkness I could see that Marie Louise was stunned by this story or perhaps by the beauty of even the slightest reflection of the poem or perhaps by our intimacy, hers and mine. I was silent for a time. The great oak tree above our heads caught the night winds; the world seemed to rock in some cradle of darkness. It was the end of a long day, and I felt perfectly at peace. "I could not believe," she said, "that he could be that happy." She wiped her eyes with her coarse cotton sleeve. "I am crying for him, that at least once he was so happy."

One morning in October of 1986, it occurred to me that I was the same age Winters had been when I studied with him. Twenty-eight years had passed. Like Winters I had become a teacher of poetry and poetry writing at a spiffy school and like him I felt like the odd man out. I lived on the ground floor of a big old house in a working-class neighborhood in Somerville, Massachusetts, with a view of the Tufts University tennis courts, which soon would be deep in snow. Except for the job I hadn't come very far. My sons had grown up, I was a grandfather twice over, and my wife and I had traveled from job to job. That morning I wrote:

> 28 years ago, faithless, I
> found the great bay of San Francisco where the map
> said it would be and crossed the bridge from Oakland
> singing "I Cover the Waterfront" into the cold winds
> and the dense odor of coffee. Before I settled
> in East Palo Alto among divorcees and appliance salesmen,
> fifty yards from the Union Pacific tracks, I spent a long weekend
> with Arthur, my mentor to be. In a voice ruined, he said,
> by all-night draughts of whiskey and coffee, he praised
> the nobility of his lemon and orange trees, the tang
> of his loquats, the archaic power of his figs.
> In a gambler's green visor and stiff Levis, he bowed
> to his wounded tomatoes swelling into late summer.
> Kneeling in the parched loam by the high fence
> he bared the elusive strawberries, his blunt fingers
> working the stiff leaves over and over. It was August.
> He was almost happy.
>
> Faithless, I had not found
> the olive trees bursting on the hillsides west
> of US 99. I knew only the bitter black fruit
> that clings with all its life to the hard seed.
> I had not wakened to mockers wrangling in my yard
> at dawn in a riot of sexual splendor or heard
> the sea roar at Bondy Bay, the long fingers
> of ocean running underneath the house all night
> to rinse off the pain of nightmare. I had not
> seen my final child, though he was on the way.
> I had not become a family of five nor opened
> my arms to receive the black gifts of a mountain road,

of ground cinders, pebbles, rough grass.
                                    At twice my age
Arthur, too, was faithless, or so he insisted
through the long sober evenings in Los Altos, once
crowded with the cries of coyotes. His face
darkened and his fists shook when he spoke
of Nothing, what he would become in that waiting blaze
of final cold, a whiteness like no other.
At 56, more scared of me than I of him,
his right forefinger raised to keep the beat,
he gravelled out his two great gifts of truth:
"I'd rather die than reread the last novels
of Henry James," and "Philip, we must never lie
or we shall lose our souls." All one winter afternoon
he chanted in Breton French the coarse poems of Tristan Corbière,
his voice reaching into unforeseen sweetness, both hands
rising toward the ceiling, the tears he held back so long
still held back, for he was dying and he was ready.

By April I had crossed the Pacheco Pass and found
roosting in the dark branches of the Joshua tree
the fabled magpie — "Had a long tongue and a long tail;
He could both talk and do." This is a holy land,
I thought. At a Sunoco station the attendant,
wiry and dour, said in perfect Okie, "Be careful, son,
a whole family was wiped out right here
just yesterday." At Berenda the fields flooded
for miles in every direction. Arthur's blank sky
stared down at an unruffled inland sea and threatened
to let go. On the way home I cut lilacs
from the divider strip of El Camino Real.
My wife was pregnant. All night we hugged
each other in our narrow bed as the rain
came on in sheets. A family of five, and all
of us were out of work. The dawn was silent.
The black roses, battered, unclenched, the burned petals
floated on the pond beside the playhouse.
Beneath the surface the tiny stunned pike circled
no prey we could see. That was not another life.
I was 29 now and faithless, not the father of the man
I am but the same man who all this day
sat in a still house, watching the low clouds massing
in the west, the new, winds coming on.

A few days later I read an unfinished version of the poem at the Blacksmith's House at Harvard, and after the reading a woman in the audience asked if Arthur were Yvor Winters. She turned out to be the poet Linda Gregerson, who had studied at Stanford after Winters had gone into the waiting cold. No one except Fran, who was there, knew that there really was a pond and a playhouse in a warren of trees, shrubs, and weeds out behind Marie Louise's great oak. I can't recall if the carp were there or not; my imagination keeps saying they belong, and my memory keeps saying, I'm not sure.

Those were two of the great gifts of truth Winters gave me. I had not known what the soul was, and so I never used the word either in writing or in speech. I tended to shy away when others used it. Perhaps that came with listening to the radio on Sunday mornings and hearing the word bandied about by professional liars. It wasn't the sort of word the old man used loosely, and when he uttered it that afternoon I suddenly knew what it meant: the soul was that part of me that left each time I lied. That day I became a spiritual man, at least until dinner. His remark concerning Henry James was no joke: he had urged me to read *The Golden Bowl*, as had Wesley Trimpi. I got the idea that Wesley thought he was a major character in the novel. I happened to mention to Winters that I'd finished the novel the night before. He asked what I thought of it. I said I was glad I'd finished it, and he asked why. I admitted that I'd hated it, that I'd read it for the wrong reason, so I could say I'd read it. Then Winters gave me his great secret truth, and I learned that truth sponsors truth.

The gift of his passion for the great dead poets was the most important thing he gave me, and since he gave it out of the deepest joy it cost him nothing. "God loves a happy giver," I once read in the Abyssinian church on top of the Holy Sepulcher, so that day Arthur was beloved of God. The last time Fran saw Winters she tried to embrace and kiss him to thank him for his many gifts to us, but he drew back, put off by such a display of affection. Perhaps in the coal camps of New Mexico he'd learned the embrace of a pregnant woman was to be feared. Perhaps not.

It's impossible to quote or paraphrase the gifts of truth I got from Marie Louise; most of them were never spoken. On occasion she could be truly eloquent even in her heavily accented English. We would pull into the gravel driveway, I would shut off the engine, my kids would leap out of the car and race toward her front porch. Behind us she would appear out of the forest of her acreage, dirt scarring her forehead, sweat running down her square, strong jaw. A hard smile would break over her face, and she would say, "This is great." All these years after, I think of her life and I think of what I caught from her, and I don't know. I do know that my friend was a woman in the deepest pain and sorrow, a woman battered by personal misfortune and by the great crimes of the century, and even on her worst days that woman was useful to me and many others. All day long she too was the happy giver God loves, the godmother to that family of five.

That family of five was not happy with the father who in August drove them to Fresno. Large with child, my wife was grumpy all the way over the Pacheco Pass and beyond. By late summer the hills were burned to a brownish yellow, the oaks leafless and lifeless, the magpies hidden in what darkness there was. Dazed summer had arrived. The holy land I'd pictured had vanished. Berenda Slough had shrunk to the size of a swimming hole; the Fresno River wasn't even a brown trickle. I stopped at an orange-juice stand on 99; the thing was a gigantic plywood orange with a big toothless mouth for service. "A piece of Americana," I proclaimed, but no one was listening. We'd left Los Altos behind and that fairyland forlorn. Everyone was mad at me. Even the four bedroom house I'd found for less than $100 a month failed to cheer their hearts. A bedroom for everyone! A study for the papa! No one cared.

The next morning I rose early and with Mark and John went out in search of a breakfast place and a San Francisco Chronicle. It was Sunday, and the town slept late. We drove back and forth down the unpeopled residential streets listening to the houses whirring, their rooftop air conditioners and swamp coolers turning over with all the life within. From each roof rose the great silver conning towers of the TV antennas. This is how you survive here, I told my boys. You close up, you grip down as hard as you can, you wait for your orders to come through the air, and you hold on. Sadly we were back in America, we were home. □

SADDLE

David Wong Louie

Ｏne day Miss Lark, her fingers nervously clasped in a bundle of knots, announced that our recital of the "Marine Corps Hymn," which had been assigned for us to learn on our plastic recorders, would be delayed a week. Instead, we were going to listen to a portion of Tchaikovsky's 1812 Overture. She gave no reason for this change in plans, but what was about to happen in the next twenty minutes would change my life, though I wouldn't know it for years to come.

Miss Lark was my elementary school's music teacher. Once a week she came whistling into our classroom, her pursed mouth like a half-eaten plum, pushing her two-tiered cart, with its turntable, records, instruments (a tambourine, wood blocks, cowbell), and songbooks. She must have been in her late twenties or early thirties back then, but she was like one of those people in vintage photos who always looked old no matter what their actual age. In her heavy cardigans, loose, beige hose, and nurse's shoes, she was a grandmother in training. With her doughy complexion, the edge of her lips permanently curled in a snarling question mark, her hair too small for her head, riding her scalp like a poodle's cut, Miss Lark was never my favorite of the roving instructors—I much preferred elfin Mr. Merry, the bow-tie-wearing art teacher or even lugubrious Senorita Murphy, her flashcards and the sorry sherbet-green suit she wore each week. Even from my nine-year-old's perspective I sensed in the out-of-proportion earnestness Miss Lark brought to the classroom a hard sadness in her being.

Before Miss Lark set needle to vinyl, she told us to rest our heads on our desks, then explained the historical circumstances that inspired the composition: Napoleon's march on Russia; the good

116

peasants' futile preparations; the assault of Russian winter; ans so on. My cheek flush to the desktop, listening to the music filtering up through the sticky wood, I was soon lulled into wonderful dewiness of vague consciousness and illicit relaxation. Even the fabulous cannons at the conclusion of the piece, though noticed, were merely heightened bursts in the steady beats of my heart.

Then it was over: the needle's abrupt disengagement, students shuffling in their seats; waking, stretching their legs. Before we were totally settled, Miss Lark told us to take out paper and write about what we had heard. I have no memory of the sorts of things I scribbled that afternoon or my thoughts about the music, but after Miss Lark collected and perused the essays, she selected mine to read to the class. I can still see the grayish sheet of blue-lined paper stretched between her pink hands, and feel my classmates' eyes embedded in the back of my head, the acceleration of my ever wilder heart racing away from me. As she read, Miss Lark's voice was milky with emotion, the sounds catching in her throat, transforming what I had written into something that sounded, at first, alien, wholly unfamiliar, something akin to song. But a few sentences in, as my words became ever more apparently just that, *my stupid words*, I felt so embarrassed—not because of what the words meant, but because they were being heard at all.

By that early stage of life—what was I, eight or nine at the time?—I had a highly developed sense of how best to negotiate the world in which my parents had dropped me: minimize how much I was seen and heard. In my kid's mind this was the surest, wisest survival strategy.

My parents came to this country from China, my father in the forties, my mother in the fifties. Neither one spoke or read English. It is fair to say that my first language was Chinese. The TV taught me English, and that blooming addiction combined with what my older sister brought home from kindergarten, formed the foundation of my ultimate conversion. I absorbed the words hungrily, like hits of pure oxygen. I was immediately transformed by the syllables, a new person born of the accumulated language. (In contrast, my parents seemed immune to it all, the talk coming from their customers, the television and the radio; they remained anchored in their past.) I remember watching TV one afternoon and saying the word *saddle*; I don't know who said it first, my siblings or I, but we were jumping up and down, delighted by the bright syllables popping from our mouths—*saddle* was like a password into a most exclusive and coveted club.

I didn't know it at the time, but I was hoarding the resources I would need one day to make my getaway. At home, I was noisy in my adopted language, each utterance like a tiny step closer to the front door. And why wouldn't I be planning an eventual escape? The whole world was inside the TV, and no one there spoke a word of Chinese, no one there looked liked my parents, no one there lived as they lived, did what they did. Despite its black-and-white unreality, everything I saw and heard on TV still was infinitely more glamorous—and enticing—than the life my parents had made for me.

This was childhood: days and nights inside a laundry; Chinese opera whining on the turntable; my parents working side by side at their respective ironing boards, rocking gently from foot to foot, their backs turned to my siblings and me, playing on the floor, the toasty fragrance of cotton slightly singed surrounding us like a shell. Our family's entire existence took place inside the store— we worked, ate, slept there. The laundry itself was housed in a freestanding building, the only structure on an otherwise-empty block-size lot, an island set off by wide streets, a sea of concrete. Our neighbors were a distant cluster of anonymous businesses. In this geographic isolation my parents worked and raised a family. They seemed to want nothing from the white world outside but its dirty laundry. Not its food, not its religion, not its language.

Based on the limited accounts they gave of their former lives in China, my parents were peasants, companions to chickens and pigs. What they came here seeking was never apparent, because the life they settled into was so lean and joyless. Making their livelihood washing and ironing other people's laundry, they shared the same destiny as everyone of my parents' friends (which led me to the inevitable conclusion that that was all they were capable of doing). Throughout the daylight hours and well into the night they labored, stopping only to eat, and in my father's case to smoke while reading the paper, and in my mother's case to cook. They sorted, washed, ironed, folded, wrapped, and stacked clothing and bedding and table linens all day and well into the night for the few pennies they charged per item. Barely a word would pass between them, nothing except short, muffled discussions of business-related matters. As for my siblings and me, we were taken care of—fed, clothed, sheltered—but rarely was I ever spoken to other than to be reprimanded, warned, or commanded. Nor was I ever touched, except when I was disciplined. In other words, my parents had as much contact with us as they needed in order to carry on with their endless chores as efficiently as possible.

It is midday, but the fluorescent tubes hanging from the ceiling have all been turned on. Outside a hurricane pounds the store. The windows are covered by dark sheets of water, condensation from the gas heater, the irons, and the temperatures of our bodies against the cold panes. My parents are close by, ironing; my brothers and I playing on the floor. In a wrestling match my dinosaur is beating up my brother's. I am dry, warm, fed. I give no thought to the storm which might easily blow the old building apart. Then the brass bell rings as the front door flies open, and the cold, damp, windy world outside rushes in. A black rainslicker enters, a white hand removes its dripping hood. His looks seem indistinguishable from the men on TV. He lays a sodden brown-paper package on the counter, the barrier that separates the customers from us. Inside are two shirts my parents had laundered and pressed. In a loud voice and with fast-sounding words he scolds my father: there is a tiny wrinkle ironed into the tip of his shirt collar, and he wants his money back! My father examines the offending garment, and showing no signs of the anger that will inevitably erupt once the brass bell signals the man's departure, he opens the cash register and picks out the dimes and pennies for his refund. I wish my father would just once yell back, slap his hand against the counter, and drown out their petty complaints, their big mouths raining their language over our heads, like a legal threat, intimidating us with their belonging.

On this and similar occasions I was disappointed by my father's failure, by his hiding his anger. I feared customers, their size, their authority, and their easy displays of fierce emotion. In fact, they all scared me, men and women, even the alleged nicer ones, who spoke with soothing voices. I hated when customers said things at me, and my parents would expect—demand—that I instantly make a response, even though they had no idea what had been said to me. I was a shy, self-conscious child anyway, and when put on the spot like that—asked to perform like a dog its tricks—my insides spun like a washing machine, my head rang empty. I could not embarrass my parents in front of the barbarian, but on these occasions my chin would drop to my chest, my boy's courage would go into hiding, and I would hurry off to the family quarters in the back of the store, the words I might have spoken lodged like swallows of fire in my throat. As soon as the customer had left the laundry, my parents would scold me for my pathetic performance; I was a good-for-nothing, top-of-the-lungs noisy with my siblings, but meek and dumb in front of the people who put rice in our bowls. They were right, and they were wrong, and I hated them.

Away from home, away from them, in the places where I was the only Chinese, I tried not to be noticed. I did not want to be recognized as their son, as one who ate with sticks, lived in the back of a store, and slept among other people's dirty socks and sheets. I was acutely aware of how others experienced their environments—I had no doubt my externalities were first and foremost in everyone's eyes. I knew every stranger's harsh opinion of me. As much as possible I showed my face to the floor or sidewalk; as much as possible, I took stingy breaths in order to minimize the piece of the world I occupied, minimize the offense some anonymous soul might take. Despite my best efforts there were still those classmates and their adult counterparts—grown men driving past in their cars or standing on street corners, idling in front of shops—who were compelled, as if responding to a deep-rooted passion, to yell insults, or call me names, or mimic the Chinese I would never dare speak in their presence, or throw stones, or spit. And dutifully I cringed, as if their taunts were hands that compacted my being and squeezed it into the tough husk of a bug. Each such act scrupulously designed to remind me who I was and what I was not: small punishments for being different, Chinese. But mostly I went blissfully undetected.

Teachers didn't call on me, the librarian didn't make me read out loud, the kids didn't pick me for their teams.

For years and years I grew fat on my own success and others' instinctive neglect: You hardly knew I was there. I occupied a seat in classrooms, I was a quiet, inscrutable friend to unpopular boys, I was a part of the visual landscape. When I did talk to people, I would replay the conversation afterwards and scrutinize every word I had said, worried I had hurt feelings or embarrassed myself in my interlocutor's eyes. Once, just before the start of a pickup baseball game, while sides were being chosen, I yelled at a boy named Danny who was slow in deciding who he wanted to play on his team. Danny was deaf, and in my impatience to get the game started I screamed something to him and everyone else within earshot about his physical misfortune. We were a bunch of boys on a baseball field; I'm not sure what Danny actually heard, though he could not mistake my angry expression or my fist smacking my palm; but the other kids did not miss a syllable, and they shoved me, told me to shut up, and patted Danny on the shoulder, asking if he was all right. How could I explain to them that I was really scolding myself for my own shortcomings, for being born what I was and would rather not be? It was the loudest I had let my voice run from me, and never had I felt an insult's sting as brutally as I did then, nor had one found its mark with greater accuracy, delivered as it was by its own target.

As Miss Lark read my essay to the class, and my little kid's neck burned with shame, cannons exploded in my chest. It snuck up on me. What I was feeling in the sound of Miss Lark's voice was the love, the gentle caress of approval my overworked parents could never find time to show. Something else also clicked: In Miss Lark's voice was my own, I was being heard without actually having to say a word. My parents—brave for their children, but not for themselves—constantly admonished me to speak to Americans in a big voice, and, in the years to come, I realized I could be the obedient son through writing. I could have a presence without being present, without making a sound. □

WALKING

Aleida Rodríguez

Today is June 10, my forty-third birthday, and I have just returned from a two-hour, early-morning walk in the Hollywood Hills with my friend Bia. We've been doing this for about ten months now, several days a week, walking and talking, looking and talking and walking. And though we have to do it around 6:30 A.M.—before L.A. heats up to a scorch and our mountaintop views of the city sprawled below become smeared with an opaque yellowish stain—getting up early is one of those small tortures one develops a palate for, having lived long enough to have experienced the significant rewards of such a small effort.

Whether we walk up the canyon toward the Hollywood sign or take the circuitous route through the neighborhood up to my favorite house, the things we encounter along the way weave themselves into our conversation. For instance, whatever's blooming at the moment—the scent of pink jasmine that makes us swoon half a block away, the Matilija poppies we've agreed look like origami eggs-over-easy. The Munchkin-like Russian immigrant couple who have finally started tilting their baba au rhum faces toward us when we greet them. The discarded condoms lying like banana slugs by the roadside (at least they're *using* them, I say to cheer Bia, who thinks her neighborhood's going to seed—so to speak). And all the birds! Dozens of different kinds we're just now learning to identify: Wilson's warblers, western tanagers, California thrashers, orioles, phainopeplas, both Anna's and Allen's hummingbirds, and, of course, scrubjays, scrubjays, scrubjays, and mockingbirds galore, each competing for the loftiest pulpit. Deer cavorting across someone's dried lawn—does anyone really live there? The various dogs: Piper, the enthusiastic golden retriever named after the champagne; Romeo, the bedroom-slipper shih tzu with a silly lock of gray over one eye; the perky corgi whose name I can never remember but which Bia insists is Hero; and all of the ones to whom we've never been properly introduced: the pair of salukis; the smooth-haired fox terrier; and the sad retriever/lab mix who lies silently on his brick step day after day, staring into the short distance.

Last week I finished teaching the last of ten sessions with a class of seventh graders at a private school in the San Fernando Valley—a stint as a visiting poet, one of several things I do to cobble together a living, along with working as a freelance editor and translator. The focus of my last class was death, or, rather, the awareness of mortality, which is different but often confused. I told them what Mr. Swanson, my tenth-grade English teacher, had told us, back in the Olden Days: "None of us get out of this alive!" he'd proclaimed in a voice like W. C. Fields, waving his arms and giving a kind of chortle. But my own students were neither amused nor charmed, as I had been—they were shocked. They accused me of being disrespectful: "This isn't a *game!*" they whined. O.K., so I *had* laughed when I'd said it, thinking they'd appreciate someone puncturing the bloated skin of the reverential. I had thought—mistakenly, apparently—they'd be as relieved as I was to have someone tell it without curlicues and pastels.

From the beginning of my time with the seventh graders, I had tried to gauge how awake they were. Did they know, I asked them (solemnly, since seventh grade is even more serious than death), that most adults look back on seventh grade as their unique, custom-made hell? Well, I didn't say *hell,* I don't think, it being a school and all; I think I tempered it and said something like *hellish.* But I was surprised at the way they tried to gloss over things, little somnambulists talking in their sleep: "This has been the best year yet." "Some people can be phoney, but you can just blow them off." "I think it's different here, because it's such a small school and everybody knows each other."

When I tried to get them to write a time-capsule document to help their forty-five-year-old selves remember what this time had really been like, they insisted they would *always* be like this, they wouldn't need to remind themselves of who they had been now, because they knew who they were and they'd *always* be like this, they would *always* love the people they loved now. "I'm not going to look back at myself now and feel embarrassed that I wore baby-Ts or watched 'Beverly Hills 90210.'" And I was catapulted back into that forever-and-ever feeling, a condition I might never have recalled if they hadn't reminded me.

For me, the future had seemed huge, but a huge warehouse filled with more of the present: the excruciating habitation of my body, my painful crushes, my separateness, my longing for connection—existing in a land of forever and ever, because that was all I had ever known and thought I would always know. But I had also started searching the books I read for clues about how to live, the kind of luxury of thought my unschooled, lower-working-class parents weren't able to indulge in, and which separated me from them even more. It was that written camaraderie—as well as movies *(The Wizard of Oz, To Kill a Mockingbird, Invasion of the Body Snatchers)* and plays (Albee's *The Zoo Story,* Pirandello's *Six Characters in Search of an Author)*—that I turned to as my true parents, giving me access to the world beneath the skin contained within the word.

Books, films, and plays were also stand-ins for experiences. My friend Peter and I walked around Culver City in all kinds of weather, taking shelter in parks and coffee shops, writing our earnest (and shitty) first poems and reading little snippets to each other, talking about people in the books we read as if they were our peers, our contemporaries, our chums. They were the ones we knew best, not the awkward or sadistic teenagers who roamed our town, but Holden Caulfield, D. H. Lawrence's Gudrun (as played by Glenda Jackson), Lord Dunsany, Oscar Wilde, Edna St. Vincent Millay, Lawrence Ferlinghetti, Doris Lessing, Sylvia Plath, Théophile Gautier, Baudelaire, Diane di Prima, among others. These friends were sophisticated. They spoke about death and love affairs and drugs and madness and the soul. And as we walked for miles and miles around our hellish little town—which, though it was attached to a major metropolitan area, felt as isolated and as ludicrous as Gilligan's Island—we fantasized aloud about the day we'd finally escape.

I was the first to leave. I had decided a long time before— from impressions gathered when the foster family had taken me along on a trip to Plymouth Rock—that Boston was the place I should go away for college. It seemed so Eastern and somber, unlike the "surfing schools" (UC-Santa Barbara and UC-Santa Cruz) a lot of the other kids were going to. Never fond of the sun—at least not the glare of Southern California—I imagined myself in a brownstone, reading a book by a radiator, the snow piling up outside a huge window through which a wonderfully atmospheric gloom sifted. Serious. Studious. Deliciously artsy in an old-fashioned sense. I thought about it so much, I began to write a play into which I projected my fantasies about going away to the Boston Conservatory of Music, where I would study theater, where it would *always* be winter.

As long as I can remember, I've been out of step with my time, never caring about the contemporary world around me but sighing wistfully over an earlier age—like the thirties. While other kids blared the Beatles and the Stones and David Bowie and Jefferson Airplane (names I barely registered), I lived on a desert island, listening to Bobby Short singing Gershwin or Judy Garland's Carnegie Hall album, in rapture over the clever, urbane lyrics. It was my love of lyrics that let me experience a brief overlap with my era in the person of Joni Mitchell, whose lyrics I dutifully memorized, following along with the text printed inside each album, sitting in the living room of our small apartment, playing each record over and over until my parents complained. To this day, I can still sing you just about anything pre-eighties by Joni Mitchell. Go ahead, ask me.

Language seemed to open a door in the air—an exit from my parents' world, where my brother's violent outbursts were becoming increasingly dangerous, and an entrance to a quiet, undisturbed planet of my own. And the arcane knowledge that because you yourself had been molecularly altered by what you'd read, you could, if you tried hard enough, reach out through the little window of the page and point out something to someone else, something you'd just seen or heard—the cardinal in the tree by your upstairs bedroom, the notes of whose song you could translate into lyrics: *I want so much, I want so much, I want, I want, I want, I want.* A simple tune, but oh so true.

That cardinal was in Springfield, Illinois, where I had been placed in a foster home to await the arrival of my parents and where, in the fifth grade, I had learned the thrilling word *simultaneous*. Being thrown into a classroom unable to speak English at age nine, coupled with living in a foreign country without my parents, awakened me to the power of language in a way that was more dramatic than if I'd lived continuously in my native Cuba, with a single tongue.

In the beginning was Eva. It was the first time I remember being conscious, absolutely aware, that something I was saying was having an effect on another person. It was exhilarating. All I knew was that I adored Eva, and that when I volunteered the spoken prayer at the end of the Presbyterian Sunday school class, she liked it. She smiled, and her full lips parting also parted, or peeled open, something in me. I shed my drab disguise as mild-mannered reporter and positively glowed. It was heady to realize that my *words*—my description of the red hibiscus bushes outside the row of arched windows, the deep blue sky beyond, the clouds like my mother's *merengues* (the first simile I remember using)—had caused her green eyes to focus on me more closely. Though I didn't yet possess the words *lesbian* or *writer,* both identities surfaced simultaneously, a process that was seamless, without any scar indicating a place of entry. I had accidentally stumbled on the alchemy of language—"Mr. Watson, come here, I want you!"—and, without knowing it, had also been initiated by eros.

Only recently, after reading Anne Carson's *Eros the Bittersweet,* have I begun to understand the role of eros in my writing. Eros—which exists in the space between lover and beloved, in the not-having—has occupied the void created by my abrupt uprooting and separation from both beloved and beloved country. Looking back over everything I've ever written, from the painfully morbid and maudlin poems of junior high to the efforts of the present, I can see there's always been a you, a me, and a third, invisible entity. If my writing has been influenced by my exile, it is in wanting to make present something that is absent, or trying to convey how fragile and fleeting everything is, because that has been my experience. And I've used language as a kind of lasso, an attempt to rope what's running away from me or, failing that, at least trace the shape of my longing in the air.

Even when I'm not addressing my exile as subject matter— and I'm not particularly interested in it *directly* right now—I still see that I write to replicate the original garden, to muse again over the dilemma of connection and disconnection, dependence and independence, before and after, trust and betrayal. To reweave the flawed fabric I've been given to wear. To dream onto the page a face that will not abandon me, that will shine back, "the third companion" that Rumi talks about in "Why Organize a Universe this Way" in *Open Secret: Versions of Rumi*, 1984:

> The third companion, what you do, your work,
> goes down into death to be there with you,
> to help. Take deep refuge
> with that companion, beforehand.

"How far does a dog run into the woods?" begins the old joke.

Try as I might to stay on the path of my origins as a writer, on the How, an unseen force keeps pulling me off into the understory of Why. It's like that last scene in *The Haunting*, where Julie Harris is finally leaving Hill House. Having said her reluctant farewells, she drives slowly away, but something takes over the steering wheel (we see her hands reach up and grasp the blonde hair at her temples as her face contorts with horror), and the car veers off into the underbrush, where we see—through the windshield, from her perspective now—the looming tree trunk against which she crashes. *How foolish it had been of her friends to think she could ever really leave Hill House!* we hear her say now in her ghostly voice. *Didn't they know that she* belonged *to Hill House—that she had* always *belonged to Hill House?*

So maybe the seventh graders were onto something. Not that we will *always* be the way we felt ourselves to be at one tiny island in time—that would deny mortality and is a mirage. But how else to communicate that deep sense of inevitability? The path we take, or which perhaps takes us, is so familiar, haven't we *always* been on it? It is ours, and we belong to it. But where will it take us?

"Halfway," goes the answer to the old joke, "because, the rest of the way, the dog is running *out* of the woods."

Having run—or walked—halfway into the woods of my life, what I have to say about how I became a writer becomes only what I can say thus far. There is no fixed point, no frozen perspective, no single entry, no clear delineation, as between meadow and wood. The scenery keeps blurring, flickering between shadow and light, enlarging, confusing my idea about *where* the woods began in the first place, and how and why I entered them at all.

I would probably offer you a different answer, or at least a different angle, every twenty years or so. When did I embark on this meandering path? Falling in love with Eva and words simultaneously at seven? Being uprooted and having to fend for myself alone in a foreign country at nine? Escaping into reading mysteries and biographies in Illinois in order to decipher the mystery of my own biography? Writing a mock Sherlock Holmes story in fifth grade ("The Case of the Strange Paintings")? Walking around Culver City, writing my derivative poems in junior high? Getting my first poem published at twenty? Winning an NEA fellowship at twenty-seven? Or maybe just in the last couple of years, when I've stopped worrying that the face shining back from the page was going to abandon me?

Depending on my mood, I could enter at any of those places and not be lying. And I'm still walking, still expanding the territory where I belong. One day, walking deeper into the woods, I'll notice my perspective has changed—the path is here, under my nose!—and I'll suddenly wonder, *When did I become the dog?* □

Do You Like It?

Kay Ryan

*H*ow a person becomes a poet is a mystery before which one must simply bow down. Perhaps one is born to it. Indeed, genetic preparations may have been underway for generations before the poet's birth. Snippings and mixings of hereditary materials may have been exactly calculated by some higher hand, one's hapless ancestors thrust together in otherwise unprofitable unions sheerly to produce the very poet one is. It could be that inevitable. It could be that grand and cruel. A person could be certifiably *called,* and of course this *is* an attractive theory, with religious overtones. It would be a ferocious religion, because so many generations would be used opportunistically, mined exclusively for their rhyme gene or their understanding of the caesura. But then, poetry *is* ferocious and opportunistic.

Or one may become a poet through an opposite process. Perhaps one is reduced to it. Instead of being the result of the refinement and purification of the blood until only poetic ichor runs, the poet may be the product of some cataclysmic simplification, much like the simplification that overtook the dinosaurs, wiping them out and leaving the cockroaches. Both cockroach and poet are hearty little survivors, quick and omnivorous.

But in any case, such speculations regarding the origin of the poet feast upon the antique and the hideous—always a pleasure, but quite unhelpful to the actual poet in youth. For this is a fact: Though a person may be absolutely destined to be a poet, the person doesn't altogether understand this at first. For a long time the person just feels silly.

It is very like the bewilderment felt by the early evolutionary predecessor of the anglerfish, back before this strange fish had undergone the "five hundred separate modifications" (Stephen Jay Gould's estimate) that it took to develop the fishing lure it now dangles before its cavernous mouth.

As in the case of this early anglerfish, the young poet feels ill-formed, but with glimmers of something yet to be articulated. This condition can go on throughout life, and, in truth, does. For how can the anglerfish ancestor jump ahead to a more satisfying form where the lure actually works? He cannot. And how can the poet evolve beyond the comical, partial creature she is? She cannot. And still, she cannot live indefinitely without forming an opinion regarding immanence and glimmers.

I wonder if other poets can say how they became poets, not in terms of the imponderably remote sources of the gift or when they got a publishing break, but can they recall a particular moment when they felt themselves say yes to the lifelong enterprise? It always surprises me that I can name such a moment. I don't see myself as a person who has "moments."   The circumstances were picturesque and dramatic in a way foreign to my desert-bred habits.

In 1976, at the age of thirty, I was bicycling across the United States. I had been feeling all the tell-tale symptoms of the poetic calling for a number of years, but was resisting it because I didn't like the part about being utterly exposed, inadequate, foolish, and doomed. Still, poetry kept commandeering my mind. So the bicycle trip was four thousand miles to say yes or no to poetry.

For a long time it didn't seem to be working.

Then came a morning, many hundreds of miles into the rhythm of riding, going up a long, high pass in the Colorado Rockies, when I felt my mind simply lose its edges. The pines swept through my mind, my mind swept through the pines, not a bit strange. All at once I no longer had to try to appreciate my experience or try to understand; I played with the phrase *the peace that passeth understanding* like turning a silver coin in my fingers. And with the peace-beyond-the-struggle-to-understand came an unprecedented freedom and power to think.

My brain was like a stunt kite; I held it by only a couple of strings, but I could ask anything, absolutely anything, of it. I tried some sample stunts, and then I asked the question: Shall I be a writer?

It was the one question of my whole life, but I asked it with no sense of weight, as though it were casual: Shall I be a writer?

I don't know where the answer came from, but it wasn't what I expected. I suppose I expected an evaluation of my talents and chances of success. What I heard was, *Do you like it?*

I had never heard anything so right. Yes; I did like it, that was all there was to it. I laughed and laughed and laughed. □

ENGLISH, MY ALLY

Octavio Solis

I never intended to be a writer. As far as I knew, my passion was for acting and for many years that was the career I pursued. Writing seemed not only incompatible with a life in the theater, but inconceivable to someone who considered the English language his worst handicap.

It's not like that ever prevented me from putting pencil to paper. From the earliest age, I can recall locking myself in my room to scribble out all sorts of nonsense. I kept a diary, I scratched out poems and stories. My mother still keeps in her old file cabinet the first two poems I penned when I was six or so: "For My Mother" and "Ode to a Prairie Dog." I wrote so much crap when I was young, and what I wrote I fancied good enough to keep, but not good enough to share with anyone else.

That's because I grew up with a lot of insecurities, due in large part to my cultural origins. I was a Mexican-American kid, born of poor immigrant parents from Coahuila, Mexico, and, for the first few years in El Paso, my brothers, sister, and I spoke a very rough and informal Spanish at home and in the streets. All the English we knew was learned from TV shows and radio. Once we got in school, we realized how woefully inadequate that was.

I gotta hand it to my teachers, though. Without ever once denying me the right to use my native tongue, they infused in me a love and respect for English which continues today. They introduced me early to real literature, to poetry with a capital P, to the fantastical worlds I thought only the movies could evoke. With a zealot's appetite, I read Poe, Verne, Twain, A. Conan Doyle, H.G. Wells, the Brontës. I wrote papers on them and later, poems and little fictions which emulated their style. It was my fifth-grade teacher, Mrs. Harris, who told me that the best revenge against those who mocked my English was to become better at it than they were. And I thought I had.

But something dramatic happened to me in high school. Recruited for the fall production of *The Diary of Anne Frank*, I discovered that I seemed to have a knack for acting. I took some speech classes, joined the Drama Club, and got cast in the next school play. In a matter of days, I was stagebit. Acting became the thing I did all through high school, and by graduation time I had resolved to make it my life's work.

Theater was a cheap and immediate alternative to the movies. The poor man's cinema, so to speak. I had long been smitten with the movies, ever since I saw from my crib the grimy black-and-white images of *King Kong* and *Frankenstein*. There was something in those old gothic horror and suspense flicks that seemed so large, so otherworldly, they were almost operatic. The theatricality of their expressions, the manner in which the world was reduced to a sound stage with stark uses of light and epic angles, and the easy insistence on the fantastic (something I later found out was called the willing suspension of disbelief), all these facets made it logical for me to drift toward the stage. Here was the same world with the same monsters, only their names were now Iago, Macbeth, and Bottom. The same beautiful, powerful sirens were there, too: Nora, Ondine, and Rosalind. Even the Mexican horror films of my youth manifested themselves in the work I saw onstage; the burlesque conflicts of El Santo and Mil Máscaras (famous wrestling idols of the fifties and sixties) battling Dracula and La Momia (The Mummy) and zombies of every ilk seemed to find their translations in the *lazzis* of commedia dell'arte and high camp. But, finally, it was the power of language in drama that drew me toward it. If I could master the English spoken by these heroes and monsters, if I could warble Shakespeare as comfortably as anyone else, then I could shed a little more of that irrational boyhood shame.

All this time, of course, I was writing and reading intensely. Working with and producing verse for the school literary magazine, I pored over the works of William Carlos Williams, Vachel Lindsay, Marianne Moore, T. S. Eliot, and Sylvia Plath. But at no time did I ever entertain the notion of pursuing this kind of work seriously. I was an actor.

Entry into college at Trinity University in San Antonio

delivered a shock to my system. Once again, I seemed to be disastrously unprepared for the level of education and sophistication that the university environment provided. Everyone spoke so intelligently, everyone seemed so worldly-wise. I could barely open my mouth to speak. I was so self-conscious of my inability with the language, and with the accent of my parent's tongue present in my speech, I really did have to frame each sentence in my mind beforehand. Actually, this acute awareness of language turned out to be an asset for me as a writer: I pay attention to the cadence of words, to the texture and coloring of each syllable, and strive to use the lexicon as a kind of music.

Of course, I was no more or less intelligent and articulate than anyone else; I was simply reacting like an insecure ESL kid from the border town. In retrospect, I think that my love for literature, which was growing more and more ardent every year, was being compromised by this strange relationship to a language I felt I had no affinity for. It was as if English was the birthright of others, not mine. Silly of me to think so, even culturally crippling, but there you have it. Whereas my mother was proud of all the English she was learning at her soda-fountain job, even poking fun at herself for the hilarious flubs she made ("Would you like a snake with that, sir?" "Are you ready for your desert?"), I was obsessing over proper usage and pronunciation and feeling alternately threatened and seduced by great works in English. This warring over the language, over its sense and meaning, continues today, albeit in a healthier mode.

If I had been exposed to the writings of people of my background, if I had at least known of Mexican-American writers like Jimmy Santiago Baca and Jose Montoya and Luis Valdez, if I had even been schooled in the rich literary tradition already established in Latin America by Gabriel García Márquez, Octavio Paz, Carlos Fuentes, and Mario Vargas Llosa, who knows how much sooner I might have turned into a writer. I hold my college partly responsible for that lapse; in the end, I should have sought them out. But I was too busy trying to become something I wasn't, hiding behind a perfectly wrought mask of erudite English. Not so ironic, then, that I should want to become an actor.

Throughout undergraduate and graduate schools, I pursued my studies in theater, focussing primarily on acting and immersing myself in as many acting styles and periods as I could. But the terms of my study required that I also take playwriting courses. Under the tutelage of such fine writing instructors as Eugene McKinney and Glenn Allen Smith, I studied scene construction, learned about dialogue, and wrote small scenes and half-baked plays. I did all this more out of a sense of obligation to my teachers than out of any desire to express myself in dramatic form. I saved that for the long self-indulgent poems I wrote in utter privacy. And, naturally, for the roles I played onstage.

It was a little weird for someone like me, a young Latino feeling diminished by his own vocabulary, to feel so comfortable speaking onstage in front of a lot of people. Only it wasn't me who was speaking; it was the people I was portraying. There was tremendous gratification in feeling the words come so naturally from my lips, fulminant and ripe and precise. I could execute any of Shakespeare's monologues; I could throw myself into Pinter and Mamet with complete command. I couldn't count on myself to be like that in real life, but in someone else's clothes, English was my ally.

Yet I never once forswore my literary bent. I took intense courses on the epic, reading and studying in two consecutive summers some of the greatest works in western literature. Among them were Homer's *Iliad* and *Odyssey*, Virgil's *Aeneid*, *Beowulf, The Divine Comedy*, *Moby-Dick*, and several of Faulkner's novels. These great works made an impression on me that, to my profit, I haven't been able to shake.

After seven years of acting courses (and as many semesters taking playwriting), I launched into my career. Audition after audition, resumes, headshots, voice-overs, readings, workshops . . . this was the routine I plunged into. Sometimes I got cast in an industrial film or a local TV commercial, and I even bagged a small speaking part in a made-for-TV movie, but generally I took part in the drudgery of dead-end auditions. It was depressing. Moreover, I began to resent being treated like meat at these cattle-calls, and I bucked at the loss of control my peers and I underwent in the process. What really rankled me, however, was the frequency with which I was sent out for roles I found demeaning: background cultural stereotypes like gardeners, waiters, butlers, and janitors. Either I was considered for these incidental parts or got cast in wretched works I couldn't recommend to my friends. These latter works often paid zero.

The single play I was proud to have been cast in was *Native Speech*, a new work by a hot young playwright named Eric Overmyer. I played a thuggish transvestite with a feral snarl and great legs. It was fun (a fucking blast, in truth) to live inside this crazy nut, but what really turned my head was the writing. *Native Speech* was full of gorgeous profane disorganized poetry, rich with metaphor and literary allusions I actually recognized; here for the first time was a play which fearlessly experimented with language and defined the universe of the characters in poetic terms; here was a work that pinned English to the mat and forced it to say shit it didn't know it could. I was aroused.

It was then that I realized: This was something I had always been dreaming about. Finally, I acknowledged this desire to write plays, plays that stretched the envelope of believability like *Native Speech*. I felt I already knew how, in some strange way. It was simply a matter of someone else showing me that it was O.K. to do so. That's when I came up with a plan to showcase myself.

I wrote a short play of about twenty minutes in length, completely in verse, employing music, song, movement, and spoken text, and I solicited the 500 Café, this Dallas nightclub where I tended bar, to let me put it on before the first music act. Once I got the O.K., I cast it, rehearsed it, directed myself and three other actors, and put it on for one night at the club. I invited directors, producers, casting directors, and local actors so they could finally see my chops in action. None of them came, but the audience that did show remarked not on my acting skill, but on the originality of the script, the word-play, the songs, the story, and even the other actors. The one question they all asked: When is the next episode going on?

So I wrote the next episode, and in the ensuing months wrote the remaining eight, presenting them every month and a half for about a period of a year. Dubbed "The Geometricia Saga," they developed a cult audience of young people, poets, dancers, journalists, and musicians (oddly, very few theater denizens), and they confirmed me as a playwright of some local stature. I acted in every one of them, but because I did double-duty as director, my roles became more peripheral. It didn't matter. I was now getting my charge from writing these phantasmagoric playlets. All the intimidation, all the alienation I had suffered from this monolith called Language was suddenly dispelled. American English was my sandbox now, and everyone wanted to play.

The most unexpected development came about when Teatro Dallas called. Their artistic director, Cora Cardona, commissioned me to write a play for her company, the only two restrictions being: 1) the work had to be set during the Mexican "Day of the Dead" and 2) its main character had to be the indefatigable Don Juan. In the first place, I was stunned that there was a company made up of Latino actors like myself, performing in pieces written by other Latino playwrights from across the country and beyond. Secondly, I was shocked that they wanted a play which reflected my own background, my culture, my own roots.

I couldn't believe my ignorance. How could I have possibly gone through seven years of collegiate study and three of professional endeavors and never once come across the works of my Raza? Never once had the notions of Latino theater and literature been introduced to me, never once had anyone suggested that perhaps I might benefit from writing closer to those bones. Now, this company was asking me to contribute to a theatrical tradition I had no inkling of.

For them I wrote *Man of the Flesh*, my first play to deal with Latino themes and characters, thus marking a new milestone in my transformation into a full-on writer. In this play, and in every work I have subsequently penned, the English I had so respected and feared was given new force and wider scope through an infusion of my original tongue, my father's Spanish. Through the further guidance of my mentor Maria Irene Fornes, a powerful playwright adept in both languages herself, I have learned to listen to the voices of the people in my plays with complete faith that whatever tongue they use will be their truest one. And they, in turn, will keep me honest in whatever language I exercise.

In attempting to mark the turning points that have made me the writer I claim to be today, I find that there was no one thing or occasion that determined my life's choice. There was always reading, always good books. I can track a graduation from one level of difficulty to another (Poe to Eliot to Joyce), and the emergence of Latin American literature as an abiding influence. Today, I am touched and inspired by contemporaries like Isabel Allende, Junot Diaz, Arturo Islas, and my favorites, Fuentes and Márquez. I still spend hours with volumes of poetry, ancient and modern, and I return to my epics as often as I can. My books were superb teachers and true accomplices in the development and execution of my craft.

But I also see that my passion for the theater helped to focus my writing. Having been an actor, I knew what an actor required; having been a director, I knew how my plays should evolve. The words I write are not meant to be read, but to be spoken aloud before an audience, under the canopy of willed suspension of disbelief. Text is simply a blueprint for something greater which lives and dies within a matter of hours each night. This ongoing sense of impermanence is what, for me, being a playwright is all about.

I see that my tutors and mentors made a difference. Even as I dallied my way through all those playwriting courses I took in college, something was being absorbed, something less about the mechanics of writing and more about the truth required to commit it. I see that Fornes pushed me to a level of trust in my own creativity, something no one had done before. She, more than anyone else, made me feel that what I was engaged in was real art. Then again, my mother made me feel that way, when I wrote that poem for her. It scanned, and it rhymed, and it danced on that sheet of paper so deftly, my mom has kept it close ever since. Her own encouragement made me a writer, too.

In the end, however, I wonder if perhaps I had always been a writer to begin with. Whatever possessed me at six years of age to lock myself in my room to scribble out poems imprisons me today behind my laptop, the door to my office firmly shut against the world. The impulse to represent myself in this manner over other forms of self-expression must have been neural at the very least. Somewhere in the back of my mind, I knew this is what I would do. No question. What is often called into question is whether I am any good at it for any length of time, but that almost doesn't matter. I write, whatever the consequences, and when I stop writing, I'll stop doing everything else, too.

Then there is this ongoing struggle with the English language. Perhaps this is what truly keeps this ESL kid from El Paso writing. It would be ironic, and, indeed, the best revenge, if the thing I considered my worst handicap should become what I'm known for. The question is, whose revenge and for what? □

WOLVES

Sallie Tisdale

*W*hen I was twelve years old, I shared first prize in an essay contest with smart Ida Egelman—what the flag means to me or something. I didn't care about the essay, the essay was a lark, a trifle. I wanted the twenty-five dollar prize, but even more, I just wanted to win. The prize turned out to be a savings bond I never saw again, but that was nothing to getting my picture in the paper. There was big homely Ida and medium-sized homely me, both of us in glasses, grinning.

I wrote short stories in those days, usually about troubled young people and their simpleton parents, in loopy, left-handed penmanship with circles over the *i*s and lots of dialogue. At thirteen I started keeping a diary ("a journal," I told my mother, "not a diary") and for many years wrote several long letters every month—self-important, soul-searching letters to match the self-important, soul-searching diary. Page after page is filled with accounts of new infatuations, rigid political beliefs, the social science theories of the teenager to whom the truth is clear though all the world is blind.

I also wrote a folk song for Earth Day called "You Should Have Seen Man Die," and a play, derivative Brechtian absurdity, at the end of which the characters discover they are really mice in a cage. I wrote a lot of bad poetry, mostly about living hidden behind a veil of tears. I wrote long complaints about being old beyond my years, hardly able to bear the hypocrisy surrounding me. I wrote about how, this time, really, I was in love. Really.

But words were just the medium. I had to balance chips on my shoulders in order to stand up straight; I'd been out of place in school from my earliest days, at odds with any form of authority.

My parents both taught and I'd spent my entire life in classrooms and teachers' lounges, slouching through empty hallways after school, waiting for my ride home, rummaging through big oaken desk drawers filled with pale gold wooden rulers, tape, paper clips, #2 pencils, the powdery pink debris of old erasers. The smell of schools is a very young memory, the sound of echoing footsteps and slamming locker doors part of my earliest environment. School, and teachers, failed entirely to interest or intimidate me.

School bored me to fury. I waded through the long, dull years by being smarter and faster than the rest of the students, by being aggressive and unpredictable and hard to read. What I really wanted was to be like everyone else, but what I cultivated was separation—apartness, the kind that needs to be noticed. I was going to be an actress; was going to do real theatre on the stage; I was going to do Shakespeare and Chekhov in modern, political revisions. As soon as I could get out of the house.

I got out of the house in 1973, when I was sixteen, too late for the revolution, but not too late to join eighty other oddball teenagers in an alternative college program called the Living Learning Center. Being thrown together in that stew of A.S. Neill and communal optimism was like winning the lottery. It was paradise. It saved my life. In L/L, students designed their own classes, shared a dormitory, and largely avoided anything smacking of the "regular" campus. Instead of Writing 101, we took Printing Techniques and Group Dynamics. We were terrible snobs.

Line by line, my journal changed, began to expand into description and idea and language-play. I wrote on the Greyhound a lot, making up stories in girlish script about my "fellow passengers" and their pitiful or mysterious lives ("43 faces, each a different picture of the American Dream and how it shatters"). I wrote short, hectoring essays on everything from environmental destruction to a dying cat. I wrote more bad poetry, plots for novels, earnest plans for communes and better sewage systems. I read those pages now and try not to flinch at the goofy quotes from Donovan and Jonathon Livingston Seagull, my refusal to use capital letters, the seemingly endless series of crushes, the deadly certainty with which every opinion is pronounced. Now and then, in the midst of this, is light: small seeds of insight and originality, tiny caraway-sized seeds buried under the weight of being seventeen years old, under the anger and sentiment and bewildered loneliness. I wasn't going to be a writer, I didn't even think about something so retiring, so slow. I was going to be a biologist, I was going to be a radical architect, a community organizer, a New Games coach. For a while I was even going to be a semanticist.

I spent a semester abroad, supposedly doing independent study. I read a great deal, alone in cold, cheap rooms, and wrote even more, sometimes for hours a day. I filled whole books with the detail of what surrounded me, with naturalistic description, with good poetry from the books I was reading instead of my own. Writing eased the loneliness at first, it was my brave, private front, but it became something more. I felt a suddenly relaxed willingness to put it all down instead of making it up. Over the course of those three months of hitchhiking and train riding and being alone, writing became the way I met the world. When I returned, I signed up for the highest level writing class I could find—"Advanced Writing," taught by an associate professor named Charles Ryberg.

Ryberg was famously cranky, with the reputation of being hard to please. Most of his upper-class students were English majors who had no choice, because the class was required for the degree. I had never been afraid, of teachers or tests or grades. I had never met a teacher I couldn't frustrate or bamboozle. The anxiety of the other students only stimulated my constitutional need to compete; I wasn't about to let a simple English teacher throw me off kilter.

So instead of naturalistic description and honest personal detail, I wrote glib and clever essays for Professor Ryberg— opinionated, mouthy stories that were perfectly serviceable, but which must have been unbearable to read. He was tall and slim and walked with an insolent stoop. He returned my essays with high grades and a slightly twisted smile. He often wore a twisty little smile, a dank and knowing smile that seemed to grow directly out of his slouch, his ninety-nine-pound-weakling body swimming slowly through the classroom with a kind of understated reluctance. "I never give anything away," he would say, mysteriously, and I believed him. I never gave anything away, either.

I started following him to his office after class, arguing with every point he made in class and with every comment he wrote on my work. That I did this seems inevitable to me now, a kind of predestined response. He was unruffled by anything I wrote or said; it made me want to impress him, because I had the feeling he was rarely impressed.

Eventually we started going to the student center so he could get a bad cup of coffee in a styrofoam cup. He drank while we talked, while, mostly, I harangued him. Eventually, he told me to call him Chuck. And eventually, I spent most of his office hours sitting in a corner simply because he never told me to leave, pretending not to listen to the conversations he had with other students and on the phone. I became his de facto assistant. I would sit in a corner of the classroom while he lectured, a tad self-importantly ignoring everyone while I wrote, self-importantly trailing after Chuck when class was done. We argued about politics and education and books we'd both read. He told me to read *War and Peace*. Instead I read D. H. Lawrence, Germaine Greer, *Zen and the Art of Motorcycle Maintenance*. In my journal that spring, I wrote, "There are few pains I haven't known."

After a few months, I started calling him the sheep in wolf's clothing. I recognized his insolence, without knowing what it was; we were both snobs, though of different types, and as we became a strange kind of friends I could see dimly that the big difference between us was that he was resigned to things. At the time, I pitied him for it. Many years later, when I understood a little why the English professor at a second-rate school is one of literature's most tragic and banal of characters, I came to envy him for it.

Once I told him to stop complaining like a cranky old man; if he hated teaching and English departments and freshman writing classes, why didn't he do something else? He gave me a funny look, with intelligence and grief in the creases of his face, but his expression was far beyond the girl I was then.

"I'm a good teacher," he said, and changed the subject.

Midway through spring term, I gave him one of my own short stories. It was the first time I had shown him personal writing, writing he hadn't assigned for credit.

A few days later, in one of our long, desultory office hours, he handed my story back; before I could read his miniature, precise scribblings, he pulled it out of my hands, flipped to the last page, pointed to the last paragraph and said, "Throw the rest out. This is good, this is where the story begins."

I started to cry, and hated myself.

Toward the end of the term, I was standing at the sale table in the college bookstore, holding a big book on Michelangelo. Even at the sale price, I couldn't afford it, but I came in every day for a week to wish I could, turning the sleek photographs with longing.

"Buy it," I heard, followed by a chuckle, and I turned to see Chuck standing behind me, slouching, laughing at me behind his glasses.

"Don't have the money," I said.

"So, *write* something, and get the money!"

He flung out his arm, impatient. *Get* the money, like that, he meant. But, what I heard was: Write something. Write. As though that was all there was to it.

It had not occurred to me to write, not like that. It had not occurred to me that one could simply *be* a writer, rather than just writing. That one could live at it.

"You think I could?" I asked, still holding Michelangelo.

He looked at me with disgust, with the familiar expression he used in class for stupid questions.

"What are you doing here?" he asked me. "You're already a better writer than me."

The next day, I borrowed money from my roommate and bought the Michelangelo book. A little later, I left that college and that town and went on to other things—other colleges, other towns. I was distracted by the world, by all that surrounded me, by my own unfinished, messy self. I got a job and lived in a communal household and volunteered for a produce collective and for a health collective and a women's center. And I kept a journal and wrote poetry and ideas for short stories, and now and then a caraway seed appeared. I traveled a little, made big plans for living abroad, learning marine biology, moving to a real commune in the mountains. I bought a bicycle and a piano and fell in love several times and got sick and got pregnant. I hardly ever wrote in my journal, but I still wrote a lot of letters, still searching my soul. I got a different job, a better job, but I never had much money. Sometimes I thought I would like to try to be a writer. I didn't know how people became writers.

One day when I was twenty-one and my son was a few

months old and I was playing the piano in the afternoon, it occurred to me that playing the piano was not going to turn me into a writer. I loved playing the piano, but I knew I was never going to be any good at it. With the solid thud of a falling rock, decision came: I sold the piano, bought a typewriter, and started writing every day while my son slept. I wrote news for a local weekly and I wrote more bad poems and stories and essays about anything I could think of, anything at all. I typed them out and scribbled on them and typed them again, sent them all out to every magazine I could find. They always came back. I scribbled on them some more, retyped them, and sent them out again.

After that, quite some years after that, I became a writer, and how I became a writer was that I kept writing.

Chuck was right, about everything. My short story was terrible, except for that last paragraph. I still have the book of Michelangelo's luminous sculpture. And I was already a better writer than he was—that is, I was that possibility, and all I had to do to be it was grow up, try harder, and get a decade of perseverance and disappointment out of the way.

I sent him a signed copy of my first book, where I'd listed his name in the acknowledgments. I was a little embarrassed, a little nervous, wondering if he had forgotten me altogether. After all, I had never so much as sent him a Christmas card in ten years. In reply, he sent me a picture of a flock of sheep guarded by a lewd and hungry wolf.

Years after that, when I had my first job as a guest professor of writing at a university with a good reputation, we had lunch. His wife laid out a fine cold lunch on the sunny balcony, and I told Chuck about the job and the fact that I was worried because knowing how to write didn't mean I knew how to teach writing. He said I would be fine, that few of my students would have any talent anyway, and most wouldn't want to be in the class in the first place, and all I had to do was talk about something I loved. "Just tell the truth and you'll do fine," he said.

"And besides," he added, brightening, smiling as a thought occurred to him. "You're going to hate English departments just as much as me." □

ADVOCATING LANDSCAPE

David Rains Wallace

*W*riting didn't appeal to me at first. After more sensible childhood daydreams of being an archaeologist or paleontologist had evaporated in puberty's glandular haze, my adolescent fantasies coalesced around art. Painting seemed an interesting, concrete pursuit—models, wine, the attractive qualities of paint itself. Writing seemed dull and abstract—typewriters and cigarettes (in those times past). I also felt, although more vaguely, that I was of the wrong social class. Writers lived in Manhattan and summered on islands off the Maine coast or in Catskills work camps. I lived in Hartford, Connecticut, the insurance capital.

My father had wanted to be a writer, but had become an industrial psychologist. His family was southern, and although he was intellectually a New Deal liberal, he kept an emotional allegiance to antebellum ideals (whatever they were). He'd been a James Branch Cabell fan at the University of Virginia, and that riffraff Faulkner's ascendancy in the late thirties had disappointed him. After the war, he left a teaching post at Tulane to become director of research for the Life Insurance Agency Management Association in Hartford. He never went back to the South. (That's not counting a year as head of software at the McNamara Pentagon—my father's background also had a military side.) I think his decision had elements of both renunciation and revenge. Once in a while, he'd talk of sending something to *The New Yorker,* but he never did.

My father's self-dislocation probably fostered my own lack of literary ambition. I grew up without feeling that I had a place or an identity to express. Connecticut was definitely a place with an identity. The old New England world remained alive in many ways. The countryside still smelled of cider mills, and we sometimes drove past a savage-looking wooded ridge where the Algonkian leader King Phillip had hidden from the Puritans. Even in town, one of the original Yankee families lived behind us, the Griswolds, who were like something out of Thoreau's gamier passages. They kept chickens. In spring, Mr. Griswold would plow his entire backyard with a wheeled contraption that looked like something advertised in an 1850 *Farmers' Almanac*. He grew Concord grapes in an arbor along our property line. I routinely stole them, regarding the half-wild, sour-centered grapes as worthless. I was astonished when he caught me one day and acted as though I'd done something wrong.

My sixth-grade school was newly built, in a place called Mooney's Woods, and every day I walked to it through a world hugely divergent from the tedium of classrooms and playgrounds. Big suckers and snapping turtles lurked under an old wooden bridge, skunk cabbage came up overnight, wood ducks exploded from hidden pools. The year before, I'd seen two whitetail does on the soon-to-be-bulldozed school site, an amazing vision in the fifties. (Deer had been extinct in Connecticut from the 1840s to the 1940s, and these were the first wild ones I'd seen.)

My father, who was always after me about what I'd learned in school, and my lack of enthusiasm for it, was himself unmoved by my enthusiasm about the does. So I didn't think that the landscape and history of a place were important, but they did seem strangely alluring. With a child's empty-headed percipience, I had discovered my father's myth—to revenge loss of identity through renunciation and repression of identity—and I was moved both to realize—I haven't been back to Connecticut since 1968—and resist it.

So I went to college intending to be a painter. A brief acquaintance with modernist formalism ended the fantasy. I'd always been an addicted reader but a mediocre English student, and in college I was surprised to find myself getting A's in literature courses. I cleaved to them. Wesleyan, which had accepted me as a local-boy underachiever, employed a lot of itinerant instructors at the time, intellectual flotsam that had drifted in from odd places— blacklisted Reds, indiscreet queers, obscure authors. One of them was a chain-smoking, gin-soaked novelist named Peter Boynton, who invited me to take his creative writing course after I'd been in his seminar on Jacobean drama. Boynton came from Hawaii and had been a military policeman—that was all I knew about him.

I wrote a story in his course about fishing trips on Long Island Sound with a friend who'd get so incensed by the trash fish called "cunners" that kept stealing the bait, that he'd start killing them in sadistic ways. Boynton said he thought I was "somebody who might become a writer." I think he liked the story because I'd described the Sound and the fish accurately. I'd liked writing the story for that reason, too, although I probably wouldn't have considered it worth writing, without the *Lord of the Flies* banality-of-evil dimension of my friend's sadism, which seemed important in the insurance-company world. (I'd found that a predictable way of getting high grades on college literature papers was to retail vaguely Camusian sentiments that I'd picked up from reading the book reviews in *Time* magazine when I was in high school: "Man's struggle against an indifferent universe," and so on.)

Writing began to seem interesting, but it took me a long time to realize what interested me about it. I continued to drift in fashionable currents. I wrote Sylvia Plath-like poetry in which the horrors of ecological phenomena like predation and parasitism played a symbolic role. This was odd, because I'd never felt that such things were particularly horrid, especially compared with what people did to each other. In the context of concentration camps, encountered on TV when I was eleven, any fear of nature seemed insignificant. Besides, I'd always found predators beautiful, and parasites ingenious, although such sentiments hadn't seemed intellectually respectable in the world of *Time* magazine book reviews. My poetry was a striking of half-consciously imitated attitudes, more of a response to partly drug-induced neurotic crises than an expression of what I thought and felt. I didn't know what I thought and felt. When the neurotic horrors stopped, the poetry did, too.

I also attempted fiction in which I managed to ignore the things that had made writing the story in Boynton's course interesting. It wasn't really fiction but thinly disguised accounts of activities pursued with the half-conscious intention of writing about them. Imitation Henry Miller, Jack Kerouac, and Thomas Pynchon. It's embarrassing even to remember that phase.

I left college without much idea of writing as something I might do in any kind of vocational, much less professional, way. I briefly pursued another fantasy—film—until the loss of a Columbia film school scholarship after very marginal participation in the 1968 student revolt left me at loose ends.

My cunner-torturing friend had become a salmon fisherman at Bodega Bay. He invited me to visit. I never got to go out on his boat, finding it broken when I arrived and my friend destitute. I had to pay his rent while he tried unsuccessfully to fix it. Instead, I took to walking around the hills, or rowing in Tomales Bay. It was a revelation—the first time I'd encountered a landscape that still had some wild megafauna attached, in the form of the harbor seals and the sea lion herds. Tomales recalled the sense of allure I'd felt in landscapes as a child.

I experienced a conversion to a state of mind that I suppose could be called Wordsworthian. Although they're ecologically different, the California coast ranges have a certain resemblance to the English Lake District—pastoral hills with scatterings of trees, gorges and crags, mists, spring wildflower displays. Such landscapes seem to have a particular resonance for the human brain. It's been suggested that they resemble African Rift Valley savanna country, where we evolved. I began to feel, and realized I'd always felt, that landscape, the earth, nature—whatever—had qualities that resonated in me. There are so many vocabularies and mythologies for this that I won't try to elaborate any here. When I say it was Wordsworthian, I don't mean I shared Wordsworth's religious beliefs—"trailing clouds of glory," etc. His best poems are good descriptions of the emotional resonance in landscape.

> There are two voices—one is of the deep,
> And one is of an old, half-witted sheep,
> And Wordsworth, both are thine!
> —"Granta," J. K. Stephen, 1891

Writing began to seem not only interesting but potentially useful, as a way to accomplish several things. It was a way of recording my feelings and observations. It "developed" them, although I dislike that term. Communicating them also seemed worthwhile. I have a normal vanity (normal for a writer, that is) about the wonders of my feelings and observations, as well as a belief that what I write about—landscape, nature, etc.—is important in itself, much too important for the treatment it usually receives from the insurance capitals of the world. By writing, it seemed that I might have an interesting time, attract others to my concerns, and get paid for my efforts. Twenty-five years later, I still don't know if those were reasonable ambitions.

Even more problematic than making a living by writing was the question of having actual political influence. I hated seeing the landscape destroyed and wanted to help protect it. The idea that my own writing might accomplish something directly in that direction didn't bulk large in my aspirations, however. I lacked the competitiveness and love of novelty that drive true journalists. This was a shortcoming, but I also felt that there are so many forces destroying the landscape that attacking particular ones wasn't enough—it was chopping off hydra heads. I set out to be an advocate for the qualities of *undestroyed* landscape.

If I was going to advocate landscape, I had to know something about it. My real education began at that point, largely pursued outside the academy. The humanities didn't have (and largely still don't have, despite many people working in that direction) an infrastructure for valuing nature's qualities, while the sciences' admirable infrastructure for valuing its *quantities* values its qualities only marginally. (I'd never even thought of taking an undergraduate biology course; in the sixties, they were all either pre-med or biochemistry—tickets to flunk out for the non-grind.) There is at least one venerable tradition for valuing the qualities of nature, however: that of natural history. A biologist can say that a landscape should be protected because it has a high diversity of species, but it takes a naturalist (often the same person) to say it should be protected because it's beautiful.

I've anointed myself a naturalist, since natural history is one of the few disciplines to retain the virtue of conferring no degrees. (People who ask if I have a "background in biology" look uncomprehending when I tell them this.) The natural-history tradition's infrastructure now lies, unsteadily, with environmental groups, museums, and government agencies like the National Park Service and its local counterparts. They've kept me going as a writer, along with occasional quick trips through the academic revolving door, usually on the humanities side. Biologists often like my writing, but biology departments seldom hire me to give readings or participate in seminars.

Almost all the writing I've done is classified as nonfiction prose, but such categories are of limited significance. My first two published books were more fictional than my derivative attempts at Pynchonesque fiction, because I used my imagination more. I was trying (based on observation) to imagine the lives of animals and plants, however, and libraries classify this as fiction only if the animals and plants are anthropomorphized—given names, speech, etc. The truth is, it takes less imagination to describe an anthropomorphized animal than an actual one. Similarly, I've used more poetic concentration and elision to get readers to sit still for descriptions of things like plate tectonics or neotenic evolution than I ever did in my dead-end versifying.

Finding a subject and a style wasn't the main problem of becoming a writer. Finding an audience was. Writers must be entertaining performers or clever politicians, preferably both. It took me three years to get a publisher for my first book, a fictionalized account of a night in a wilderness area. Then, for each new book, a new audience had to be found. Since 1980, television shows like "Nature" have ended the market for the kind of writing I did in my first book. Why imagine what it's like to be a jumping spider feeding on a gnat when you can actually see the devouring itself, at least as it was filmed in a studio?

The West Coast was good for the kind of self-education I was pursuing. Landscape and society were not yet stacked into mutually oblivious strata, as in Hartford. This was largely because the West Coast's mountainous, semi-arid, tectonically active landscape is harder to ignore than the East Coast's more humid and quiescent one. Still, there aren't many other places where wilderness is a day's travel or less from major museums and libraries, and this had produced at least a small literary tradition of paying attention and respect to landscape, a tradition I learned to—participate in? appropriate? I moved in and set up shop anyway, not always welcomed by the natives. A bioregionalist of repute once came up to me and, by way of introduction, said: "I don't like your style."

In fact, I'm not a regional writer. I don't have roots on a ranch or a reservation, as New York publishing requires of fully accredited western writers. (I'd never have been able to *be* a writer if I'd had to depend on New York publishing.) My writing about the West Coast has been the most successful, largely because West Coast tradition has provided an audience for it, but I've written as much about the East Coast and Central America. After I learned about the West Coast, I had to go back and learn about the eastern natural history with which I had ignorantly grown up. Then I had to go and learn something about the tropical natural history with which I had, in an evolutionary sense, ignorantly grown up. (I think all humans should have a chance to experience tropical forest and savanna, a kind of eco-evolutionary *hadj*.)

The concept of region is a fairly arbitrary one, anyway. A blacktail deer's region may be a watershed; a Swainson's hawk's is a couple of continents. I don't see allegiance to region as my reason for writing about places. I'm still not sure why I write about places. In my more anthropomorphic moods, I sometimes think it's because they call me to write about them through an esoteric network of chance encounters, dreams, and visions. In my more—what, zoomorphic?—moods, I think it's just because, like Sir Edmund Hillary's Everest, they're there, and I'm here, a bit of mind drifting through the biosphere.

> Into the universe, and why not knowing,
> Nor whence, like water willy-nilly flowing,
> And out of it, like wind along the waste,
> I know not whither, willy-nilly blowing.
> —*Rubáiyát of Omar Khayyám*
> Edward FitzGerald trans., 1859 □

PRINTER'S INK IN MY VEINS

Peter Booth Wiley

*I*f I had ever taken the time to look at the pale underside of my wrist when I was in one of those heightened states, I might have noticed that my blood runs darker, that there is a touch of printer's ink in my veins inherited from the five generations of my father's family who were intimately involved with the publishing of books. I guess this means that I was born with the book person's equivalent of the proverbial silver spoon. I had one of those too, neatly monogrammed, along with a little cup, which my mother acquired as a measure of the social distance she had travelled from her family's farm on Long Island to the home of a successful publisher.

So I grew up literally surrounded by books. My siblings and I were read to from the choicest children's literature on my parents' comfortable sleigh bed — *Wind in the Willows, Tom Sawyer, Treasure Island, Robinson Crusoe* and a curious set of period pieces called the Lawrenceville stories about young preppies with wonderful names such as Dink Stover, the Prodigious Hickey, Hungry Smeed, and the Tennessee Shad. My father was the principal reader, and, if anything, he enjoyed these tales more than we. I still remember when I first read a book on my own from beginning to end. It was *Clear for Action,* a story about press gangs and seafights during the War of 1812. The shelves in our living room were filled with books on politics and history, popular literature, classics, and *Life's Picture History* of this and that. There was another shelf of books in the bedroom I shared with my brother, and we slept on either side of a cabinet that contained, first, the *World Book,* and then, the *Encyclopedia Britannica.* Eventually, when my parents bought a larger house, they filled it with books. There were books everywhere: bookshelves in bedrooms, in hallways, in the guest room, stacks of art books on the coffee tables in the den and living room. I still live my life in the same way—surrounded with books.

Even though I grew up with books, I should note that the family business was scientific and technical publishing. My great-great-great-grandfather, Charles Wiley was the founder of the company. He was really a printer as no distinction was made between printing and publishing in 1807. Charles was James Fenimore Cooper's first publisher, and his son, John Wiley, who gave the firm his name, published the first works of Hawthorne, Poe, and Melville. But we suppose, from the little that we know, that John was a failure as a literary publisher. Or perhaps writers steered clear of him after he censored Melville's *Typee*, forcing him to remove his critical comments about the activities of missionaries, whom John Wiley very much supported, in the South Seas. Influenced by his sons, one of whom was an engineer, John decided that scientific publishing made sense in a rapidly industrializing America. At the time of his death in 1891, there was only one remaining vestige of his literary interests, the continuing publication of the works of John Ruskin.

My father joined the firm in 1932 and became the fifth descendant of Charles to head the company. Although he was a voracious reader who consumed both good literature and lots of history, we did not socialize with the New York literati. We entertained and were entertained by sci tech publishers, a number of them in Europe. The distance between my father's vocation and my own reading interests probably created something of a barrier between me and a clear path to the world of books. I don't have a particularly scientific or technical mind and have learned to understand these matters through reading their history. I wondered wrong-headedly whether, as a person with a passion for history and literature, I had a place in the worlds of science and technology.

For this and other reasons, it did not occur to me for years that I wanted to be a writer. The curious thing is that I pursued the craft unwittingly. I wrote and published, but never as a writer, always in my mind as something else. My brother and I put out our first publication when we were probably ten and twelve after our parents gave us an old Royal typewriter. We painstakingly typed up one copy of a family newspaper, *The Wiley Herald*, struggling to give it a masthead and to keep the articles in columns. I have a vague image of a lot of straggling, typed-over words, some with broken letters, but can't remember what we covered: what we had for dinner; the activities of Barry, our Dachshund? It is all lost to time.

I was privileged to go to a struggling progressive school, which was housed in two, long, barn-red buildings with tall double-hung windows in the woods of New Jersey. Far Brook emphasized the arts in an effort to develop "the whole child." The school was obviously influenced by the works of John Dewey, though the director, perhaps responding to the intolerance of the fifties, made a point of saying it was not a progressive school. This was my most formative educational experience, the one that far outweighed others in shaping my interests and intellect. Surely the rest of my educational experience was important, a private and very traditional boy's country-day school, a prestigious northeastern college, and a large midwestern university, but Far Brook with its little library sequestered in a small, shingled cottage where there was a fire on the hearth on winter days, was a kind of children's utopia.

We were encouraged to write creatively, and we had one teacher who was particularly inspiring. Her name, which we loved to intone, was Anna Maria Louisa Perrott Rose Wright. She wrote young adult books using most of her names. She was a large, gray-frocked woman, glasses hanging from a chain around her neck or pushed back on her head on top of a long hank of coiled graying hair. She read to us, and I particularly remember the *Chanson de Roland*. I have no recollection of anything that I wrote or that writing was a particular joy. I was more drawn to sports and the woods.

Far Brook in many ways was organized around its regular theatricals: a harvest processional at Thanksgiving, a rendering of the Christmas masque based on the Gospel of St. Luke, and a springtime production of either *The Tempest* or *A Midsummer Night's Dream*. I must have been judged an actor of limited capabilities. I did get to be the narrator for the masque one year. I love the words that I read from St. Luke: "And it came to pass in those days that there went out a decree from Caesar Augustus that all the world should be taxed. . . " so rhythmic, so orotund. I was Joseph another year—getting a lot of embarrassing laughs when I had to say, "Joseph had a grizzled head." I was never offered a part in a Shakespeare play, but I was exposed to our great oral tradition at a tender and impressionable age.

There was one other event at Far Brook that came back to puzzle me in later years. We spent a lot of time studying ancient Egypt, Greece, and Rome, even taking Latin, which I continued to study and which would cause some problems with my own writing later on. But I have a very distinct memory of laboring over a map of Indochina, so that when I became aware of the war in that part of the world almost a decade later, something that would *compel* me to write, I already knew that there were a Cambodia, Laos, and Vietnam. Why was this? It might have been about the time of the French defeat at Dienbienphu, but really I have no explanation.

In high school I accepted the job of sports editor on the school newspaper, partly because of the camaraderie of the small office where we could work without interference from faculty members. We also were permitted to leave the campus, after signing out at the front office, of course, for regular trips to the printer in downtown Elizabeth, New Jersey, and a stop at the soda fountain for an Awful-Awful on the way. (When we were younger, my father had taken us to a printing plant, and I was fascinated by the linotype machines where the long, gray lead bars were lowered into a melting pot, from which the molten lead flowed into molds and appeared as type, slugs of which we took home with us. And the presses themselves were simply overwhelming, huge rolls of paper screaming through web after web to emerge as the printed page.) At the printers in Elizabeth, I would stand mesmerized, watching the linotype operators bang away, sniffing up the odor of hot lead, not knowing, of course, that they were frying their brains. Printing was alchemy, the way in which the insubstantial stuff of one's mind found its way between two hard covers.

When I thought of a vocation in high school, I considered publishing for a quick minute and then fastened for a time on the ministry for a curious and timely reason. I went to a high school religious conference where I heard Yale chaplain William Sloane Coffin talk about the Freedom Rides in the South. Coffin was a powerful presence, and I wish I remember what he said, but I don't. All I know is that he unsettled my mind. I had been brought up an Episcopalian of a middling type attending a shabby, barn-like church in the small town where we lived. I took religion seriously.

I sang in the choir and then became an altar boy, struggling to make it through the long communion prayers on my knees. Coffin suggested another kind of religion, one that responded to the disturbing events that were taking place outside the self-absorbed world of suburbia.

Like any teenager, I was a bundle of contradictions. I was callow and conventional, an eager preppie, a jock, an admirer of nice clothes, a beer-drinking party boy who pursued young women knowing very little about what to say once I had finally captured one. But there was something else there that made me increasingly uneasy around the comforts, insularities, and prejudices of suburban New Jersey. For one, I had seen the worst that America had to offer on my uncle's Long Island farm. I worked with him one summer picking and grading string beans and helping to manage a crew of black migrant workers. For a number of years he hired the same crew, because unlike other farmers he provided them accommodations, a single, two-story farmhouse, for thirty or more people. Some lived in the house, others in their cars or in or under their trucks. This crew came back to work for my uncle year after year, because these accommodations were better than the alternative. The rest of the migrants lived in camps—one for blacks, one for Puerto Ricans—which were little more than sheds surrounded by the naked earth. They had that concentration-camp look about them. I had absorbed some strong moral lessons from Christianity only to find that the world didn't work that way.

From the suburban cocoon I unwittingly went into deeper isolation at Williams College nestled in the hills of western Massachusetts. But even Williams, then a venerable drinking establishment with bright students but few intellectual pretensions, was touched by the larger social issues. Inspired by an English instructor, I began to read *The Nation*, *The Partisan Review*, *The Realist*, and the left press, and then the Marxist and neo-Marxist classics and books on Cuba, China, the Soviet Union, the labor movement, utopian communalism, the economy, etc., etc. It seemed like I spent more time reading on my couch than I did preparing for and attending classes. It certainly showed in my mediocre grades.

In the spring of 1961, in the glory days of the Kennedy administration, a handful of us went to Washington to demonstrate against nuclear testing. We even marched down fraternity row, a pathetic little band made up of students and faculty wives, jeered at by the frat boys. We didn't care. Under the leadership of the captain of the football team, some of us were circulating a petition to abolish fraternities, which is what ultimately happened. Another handful of students organized a support group for the civil rights movement. Meanwhile, I was reintroduced to Vietnam when I wrote a paper on Laos for a political science class probably in the same year. As the war escalated, we picked up bits and pieces of information from the left press and, finally, when they began to cover it from the established media, while we carefully scanned student newspapers from Harvard, Michigan, and Swarthmore to see what was happening with regards to the civil rights movement and the war on those campuses.

I struggled with my academic writing. Papers were torture. I would slave away, barely able to produce the requisite number of pages, all of them written in a ponderous style that I picked up translating Cicero in high school Latin classes. The one time that I wrote freely was in a course given by a British labor party intellectual. We were asked to write a paper on Hannah Arendt's *Totalitarianism*. I quickly dismissed her work and launched into a free-flowing exegesis on the relationship between traditional Marxism and the national liberation struggles in Cuba and Vietnam. My efforts were not appreciated. I tried writing for the college newspaper, doing a long piece on faculty attitudes toward the House Un American Activities Committee. I knew about the anti-HUAC demonstrations in San Francisco, and a group of us had invited Congressman James Roosevelt to the campus to talk about his campaign to abolish HUAC. Fewer students than could fill a small dormitory living room showed up, and I found the faculty to be strangely reticent and obtuse when I interviewed them. But even writing for the school newspaper was more than I could handle. I wrote a couple more pieces and then settled into a copy editing job. My struggle with writing had become so bad that I even accepted a kindly roommate's offer to draft a paper for me.

In my senior year, 1964, the same roommate, a fellow radical, which is what we were calling ourselves by then, was the editor of the college paper. We were faced with what to do when it was announced that Secretary of State Dean Rusk, a fervent supporter of the war in Vietnam, would be presented with an honorary degree at our graduation. There was no chance that we could get more than four or five people to demonstrate. So we staged a demonstration...in the paper. We made some picket signs and photographed three or four graduates in their robes marching in front of our dorm and ran it on the front page of the paper. We all left town the same day, never looking back.

I was fixed on an academic career, naively unaware that that meant writing as well as teaching. I was drawn to the University of Wisconsin for graduate studies because of the work of historian William Appleman Williams, one of the founders of the revisionist school of new left historians. But the summer before, I went south to work as a community organizer in the coal fields of Eastern Kentucky. It was time to put all the undergraduate chatter about the need for a popular social movement—inspired by civil rights activism, people spoke of the interracial movement of the poor— to the test of action.

In the narrow hollows of Perry County, I found an unknown world of deep forests, impoverished families living in weather-beaten shacks, smoldering slag heaps, and hillside gardens that looked like they could only be plowed by mountain goats. Perry County was soft-coal country, where miners had literally gone to war to build a union, John L. Lewis's United Mine Workers. And now, with the connivance of the UMW, the coal operators had all but broken the union. To protect their contracts in more productive coal fields, the union had agreed to abandon southern Appalachia, even selling off the chain of hospitals that had been built throughout the region with the miners' sweat and blood. Starting with a series of futile strikes in the late fifties, local miners had mounted an effort to protect their contracts, which led to the formation of a local organization known as the Roving Pickets, because of their practice of moving from mine to mine in heavily-armed car caravans. By 1964, there was one union mine left in Perry County and another in the adjacent and more notorious Harlan County. The leaders of the Roving Pickets had been indicted on state charges of assaulting scabs and federal charges of attempting to dynamite a railroad bridge that led to a mine that was once unionized. At the urging of some local lefties who had provided support for the Roving Pickets, a defense committee was formed in New York, and students were recruited for a summer of organizing work inspired by the civil rights movement's activities in the Deep South. In Kentucky we focused on building local organizations that could compete with the courthouse politicians to gain control of the funds that were being funneled into the area through Kennedy's Appalachian Redevelopment Program.

I moved in with the family of a disabled coal miner. Rich's sciatic nerve had been damaged when rock fell from the ceiling of a mine leaving him pinned to the ground until someone found him at the end of his shift. To stimulate the nerve and relieve the constant pain, he was on a steady diet of cigarettes and coffee. Haggard, thin, and lined, he looked twenty years beyond his age. But he could still plough behind the family mule in their hillside corn- and-bean patch. Rich and his wife Ollie ran a tiny store in a community of about ten houses. Because of the large number of break-ins, they and their four children slept on mattresses in the store, while I had the house, two rooms and a kitchen, to myself. Fascinated by the no-nonsense toughness, resilience, and dignity of my new friends, I began to take notes describing organizing meetings, strategy sessions, families, and residences. We were also working on two trials simultaneously. So I was sent off to Lexington as a sort of guardian for seven of the eight federal defendants who were charged with attempting to dynamite the railroad bridge. We moved into a skid-row hotel that doubled as a whorehouse. I paid for room and board and made sure that my charges made it to court every day. No nights out on the town! We ate at the shabby café next door, where my wards' favorite jukebox tune was a somber ditty called "Stone Walls and Steel Bars." At night we sat on our beds telling stories, while two of the men cleaned their pistols.

Encouraged to write an article, perhaps for *The Nation* or some other political journal, I sat in court day after day taking notes. Two of the men had been caught in the act of placing dynamite and nitroglycerin on a bridge. Five other defendants were tied to the scene by alleged confessions. One defendant was an add-on; he was a gun-runner who had shot and wounded the Hazard police chief in an unrelated confrontation. He had been added to the list of defendants apparently to satisfy the police chief's need for revenge. I took pages of notes, but had no idea how to shape this incredibly rich material into a publishable article. Easily discouraged, I put my long draft aside. I did write a piece for the Williams alumni magazine—an interesting choice—and went on to write my master's thesis at Wisconsin on the UMW. I had signed up for the summer, but found it hard to cut my ties with Kentucky when it came time to go to graduate school. Ultimately, I was a duck out of water, a well-intentioned middle-class adventurer wandering through an alien landscape. In three months, Kentucky had provided an education that was virtually unobtainable in any academic setting, and I have always hoped that I gave back at least an iota of what I took away with me. One thing was clear, if only in retrospect: events were compelling me to write.

I was sitting in a barber shop in Hazard in August, 1964, when I picked up the Louisville *Courier-Journal* to find that our government was bombing North Vietnam. In graduate school, I threw myself into work with the anti-war movement, as the war gradually escalated and I began to face the possibility of my own tour in Southeast Asia. Meanwhile, I arm-wrestled my thesis, banging away at my little green portable typewriter.

In 1967, the university planned a celebration for the 50th anniversary of the Marshall Plan. For anti-war militants it was one more opportunity to harass the government officials sent to participate about Vietnam. We knew little about the Marshall Plan and less about Greece and Turkey, where the first aid was distributed. A few weeks earlier, there had been a coup in Greece. A group of colonels acting with CIA connivance had ousted Andreas Papandreou, a moderate leftist who had once been a professor at the University of California. Here was more grist for the political mill.

I talked with two Greek opponents of the regime who showed up at the conference and then began digging into Greek history. I found that the Marshall Plan was purportedly designed to combat "communist aggression," but the story was infinitely more complicated. The U.S. had come to the rescue of a repressive regime riddled with Nazi collaborators who were trying to rid the country of an indigenous leftist movement that had led the resistance to the Nazis. Greece, it turned out, was the first instance of the use of American napalm against a guerrilla movement. I wrote a two-part series for the local underground newspaper and began to contemplate a future as a radical publisher.

My brother and I spent hours poring over plans and drafting a proposal to launch a political journal. Graduate students working with William Appleman Williams had founded *Studies on the Left* in

1959. But most of the original contributors had moved on, and we found the magazine too academic, divorced from the myriad organizing activities that its writings had helped inspire. The *Studies* crowd was ten to twenty years older than our peers, who were activists to the core, if not entirely thoughtful about what they were doing. Indeed, our elders often dismissed us as insufficiently theoretical and analytical about our work. The new left, we thought, needed an analytical review that could bridge the gap between theory and practice by looking not only at the political economy but at the successes and failures of what we called The Movement. In retrospect, I am bemused by our obvious lack of editorial and business skills. But these were willful times, and there was a panache to our go-ahead naiveté that encouraged us to plough through obstacles that would have daunted more reasonable people.

In 1968, I moved with my wife and daughter to San Francisco, where my brother soon joined us. We saw San Francisco as a good place to find writers and readers for our new journal. I continued to hold on to the idea of pursuing an academic career, but was increasingly preoccupied with the proposed magazine and anti-war work. By 1969, we had put together an editorial collective and merged our efforts with an existing New York-based magazine, *Viet Report*, to launch *Leviathan*. It was an instant success, which was not surprising given the explosive growth of the student movement in those years and the huge demonstrations against the war. Our offices were in bohemian heaven, ensconced with a group of black arts organizations in an old photo-processing warehouse behind the Opera House. The roof leaked during one of the worst rainy seasons in years, leaving puddles on the floor. The furnace, when it worked, barely took the chill off the place. Our offices were little more than crude wallboard and two-by-four partitions lined with shelves, which we built from lumber that we scavenged from an old, burned out opera house in the area. And there were creepy people visiting and living in the building, including a man who died of an overdose on the top floor. But the building fairly burst with creative energy. There were poets, dancers, actors, a comic book publisher, two newspapers, and God knows how many other activities. Most important, it was a place of our own making, and every day seemed to put us in touch with something new, as young lefties came from Asia, Europe, and Latin

America to meet us.

At the time, I saw myself as a publisher and editor, but most of all as an agitator. I wrote occasionally for *Leviathan,* often choosing subjects that our editorial collective thought should be covered, but could not find others to write. I became particularly fond of research and fancy that my articles were well grounded in facts and clearly argued without the uses and abuses of Marxist jargon. To our credit, we successfully maneuvered around the shoals of infantile sectarianism for a time, but many of the key members of the collective felt compelled to give up editorial work for organizing. There was little tolerance for arm-chair theorists. The collective dwindled to three persons, and we ceased publication.

I was already working for an anti-war newspaper written for active-duty servicemen. Here the writing was quite different: punchy articles in accessible language, but with a high premium on providing solid information about the war. Acting as a kind of international news service for the GI press, we exchanged papers with the dozens of anti-war newspapers started by American servicemen and their civilian supporters here and abroad. We shipped bundles of papers to Vietnam using Armed Forces Post Office addresses in San Francisco, took others to sympathetic stewardesses who worked the charter flights between Travis Air Force Base and Vietnam, and handed out hundreds more at the San Francisco Airport, the Oakland Army Terminal, Alameda Naval Air Station, and along Market Street where the USO was located.

When the Paris Peace Accords were signed in 1975, I, like many of my cohorts, was left in limbo. For six years I had been a journalist-agitator, but had no profession in a conventional sense and no contacts with the "real" world. My marriage was faltering. I had no idea how to make the jump from the vanishing world of The Movement to the world of a nine-to-five job. I felt a sense of obligation to the family business, but did not know how to fit into that enterprise or even if I wanted to. Disoriented and often depressed, I applied for a job as a community outreach worker in a mental health program in one of the city's black neighborhoods. The interviewers looked at my résumé—Williams College, B.A., University of Wisconsin, M.A., etc.—and asked if I was lost. Instead of puffing myself up with indignity and firing back a reply about my organizing experiences, I folded and went home.

I took a job driving a cab. I needed time away from brain work to sort things out. Note that during all this time, I never considered myself a writer nor even considered going into a journalism career. What was I going to do? Take my collection of clippings from the left press to an interview at one of the local newspapers, both of which seemed about as sympathetic to lefties as the *Wall Street Journal*? Driving a cab was a kick. The drivers were fascinating, the customers a blend of the weird and wonderful. We had the run of the city, and the pay was reasonable. But I did not plan to be a cab driver for the rest of my life.

I no longer remember how I found my way back to Pacific News Service. I had witnessed its formation in the sixties by Franz Schurmann and Orville Schell, two eminent China scholars, who opposed the war in Vietnam, while using the clippings files in the office of their parent organization to put together information packets to send to GIs. Franz and his wife, Sandy Close, were reshaping PNS, which began as an anti-war service focusing on Asian issues, into a general-interest news service that took an iconoclastic view of world events, but was less associated with a political movement, which, in any case, no longer existed. I started an investigative piece that detailed the deals that San Francisco Mayor Joe Alioto was cutting for family and friends along the waterfront. I got bogged down in research, never really thought to interview anyone, and handed in four or five thousand words. That's nice, the editor responded, but we were thinking more of a thousand words. Without any training in journalism, I didn't even know what a lead was. Even so, PNS kept me on, providing an encouraging atmosphere, free-form and chaotic, but inspiring. Over time, as I wrote more and more stories, I began to get the hang of what I was doing. But I was clearly not headed for a Pulitzer and didn't really think of making the jump to the established media.

At PNS I began to think about a book that would revisit some of the questions my earlier research had raised about Vietnam. I had written an article for *Leviathan,* "Vietnam and the Pacific Rim Strategy," which was widely reprinted and even got me invited on a speaking tour in Australia. In it I examined the links between global corporations based in San Francisco, such as the Bank of America and Bechtel, and the projection of U.S. power into the Pacific Basin after World War II. This was 1969. In the seventies, the established press began to talk about the Pacific Rim and the Pacific Basin. I knew that corporate leaders had been considering various regional strategies since the early sixties and probably earlier. But why? What was it about the development of the political economy of the American West that had led to the expansionist urges that took us to Vietnam? Good questions, but how was I, who struggled through thousand-word pieces, going to write a book?

The answer was that I would work with someone else who knew about writing books. I had met Bob Gottlieb during the *Leviathan* days. Now, in one of those fortuitous developments, we met again through a mutual friend. During a walk on the hill above my house, we talked about our various writing projects, and he proposed that we write a book together. Bob had just co-authored a book on the Los Angeles *Times*, which David Halberstam would pick clean for information for his more widely read *The Powers That Be*. Bob had an agent and a publisher, and he knew how to write a book. Some time during the years at PNS, I realized that I wanted to be a writer. I was thirty-five, and I began to call myself a writer.

Bob and I set off on several years of adventures during which we wrote two books—both investigative works, one on the major cities of the arid West, the other on the Mormon church— numerous magazine and newspaper articles, and finally started a newspaper column. I mastered the investigator's skills, learned to delicately extract information from interviewees, and how to churn out words at a steady clip. *Points West* was a hand-to-mouth operation. We wrote the stories, got them copied, addressed the envelopes, licked the stamps, and collected the bills. The column was successful enough with some thirty papers running it at one time or another. We even wrote a handful of op-ed pieces for the *Wall Street Journal,* after being drafted by an editorial-page editor who was looking for left-of-center views from the West Coast. We were looking at the region in ways that no one else was, or at least we hoped that was what a major newspaper would realize. We turned to two California newspapers hoping that one of them would buy the column from us and put us on staff. Then we could focus on our writing, get our expenses paid, and not worry about the pitiful amount of money that we were making. We liked to call this our Silicon Valley strategy, maybe because I was actually working in a rented room off a friend's garage. We'd built a viable product. Now we were going to sell the company to the big guys. Except the big guys were not interested.

Bob and I parted company amicably. I tried to keep the column going for a while, but my heart was not in it. At about the same time, I was asked to join the board of my family's publishing company and found myself flying back and forth between San Francisco and New York learning how to deal with the problems of a very troubled business.

I also began to explore the prospects for a book I would write myself. I spent three years researching the story of the U.S. naval expedition that persuaded the shogun at the end of deck-mounted swivel guns to forgo his ancestors' historic policy of refusing to deal with the outside world. It was an epic sea story resonating with all the themes that would reappear in Vietnam. The writing—narrative history, descriptive passages, character development—challenged and satisfied me, and I felt at the age of almost fifty that I was a solid midlist writer with more books than I could ever write ahead of me. I had mastered the fundamentals of my craft, but recognized that it would take years more work to attain the highest levels of word-smithing. And I was still an agitator at heart.

I never studied biology, but I once heard a student say, "Ontogeny recapitulates philogeny." I didn't know what he meant. I just liked the rhythm of the words, and they stayed with me. The origin of the individual organism recapitulates the development of the species. It would seem that this was my case. A person born of a book family inevitably finds his way home. Perhaps this would have been the case in any era, but in the years between the first civil rights sit-ins and the Paris Peace Accords, I was compelled to write not by genetics, but by events in the larger world where I found my own ways to use the written word. □

NOTES ON CONTRIBUTORS

Opal Palmer Adisa was born in Jamaica in 1954 and now lives in Oakland, where she is an associate professor at the California College of Arts & Crafts. Her most recent book is *It Begins and Ends With Tears* (Heinemann Press, 1997).

Sheila Ballantyne was born in Seattle in 1936 and now lives in Berkeley. She is an associate professor of English at Mills College in Oakland. Her most recent book, a collection of stories, is *Life on Earth* (Simon & Schuster, 1988).

Bill Berkson was born in New York City in 1939 and is now a poet, art critic, curator, and a professor of art history at the San Francisco Art Institute. His most recent book of poems is *Lush Life* (Z Press, 1984). E-mail: berkson@sirius.com

Jon Billman was born in Rapid City, South Dakota, in 1968 and now lives in Kemmerer, Wyoming. His first book, a collection of stories, is *When We Were Wolves* (Random House, 1999). E-mail: billman@hamsfork.net

Justin Chin was born in Malaysia in 1969 and now lives in San Francisco. His most recent book is *Mongrel: Essays, Diatribes & Pranks* (St. Martin's Press, 1998). E-mail: sloth3@slip.net

Blair Fuller was born in New York City in 1927 and now lives in San Francisco. A co-founder of the Squaw Valley Community of Writers, his most recent book is *A Butterfly Net and a Kingdom* (Creative Arts Books, 1989).

Jewelle Gomez was born in Boston in 1948 and now lives in San Francisco, where she is the executive director of the Poetry

Center and American Poetry Archives at San Francisco State

University. Her most recent book is *Don't Explain* (Firebrand Press,1998). E-mail: jewelleg@sfsu.edu

Forrest Hamer was born in North Carolina in 1956 and is now a psychologist in Oakland and a lecturer at UC-Berkeley. His first collection, *Call & Response* (Alice James Books, 1995), won the Beatrice Hawley Award. E-mail: FHamer8580@aol.com

Adam Hochschild was born in New York City in 1942 and now lives in San Francisco. He teaches at the Graduate School of Journalism at UC-Berkeley. His most recent book is *King Leopold's Ghost: A Story of Greed, Terror, and Heroism in Colonial Africa* (Houghton Mifflin, 1998).

Ginu Kamani was born in Bombay in 1962 and now lives in Corte Madera, California. Her most recent book is *Junglee Girl* (Aunt Lute Books, 1995). E-mail: jungleeji@aol.com

Dorianne Laux was born in Augusta, Maine, in 1952 and now lives in Eugene, Oregon, where she is an associate profesor and the director of the University of Oregon's Program in Creative Writing. She co-wrote *The Poet's Companion: A Guide to the Pleasures of Writing Poetry* (W.W. Norton, 1997). Her new collection, *Music in the Morning*, will be published next year by BOA Editions. E-mail: dlaux@darkwing.uoregon.edu

Philip Levine was born in Detroit in 1928 and now lives in Fresno, California, where he is retired from California State University. His most recent book is *The Mercy* (Knopf, 1999).

David Wong Louie was born on Long Island, New York, in 1954 and now lives in Venice, where he teaches at UCLA. He is the author of *Pangs of Love* (Knopf, 1991), a collection of stories, and the forthcoming novel, tentatively titled *The Barbarians Are Coming*, due out early 2000, from GP Putnam & Sons, Inc.

Aleida Rodríguez was born in Cuba in 1953 and now lives in Los Angeles, where she works as a freelance editor and translator. Her first collection of poetry is *Garden of Exile: Poems* (Sarabande

Books, 1999). E-mail: AReditor@pacbell.net

Kay Ryan was born in the San Joaquin Valley in California in 1945 and now lives in Fairfax, California, where she teaches basic English skills at the College of Marin. Her most recent book is *Elephant Rocks* (Grove Press 1996).

Octavio Solis was born in El Paso, Texas, in 1958 and now lives in San Francisco. Four of his plays have been published, most recently in *More Plays from South Coast Repertory* (Broadway Play Publishing, 1998). E-mail: octavios@flash.net

Sallie Tisdale was born in Yreka, California, in 1957 and now lives in Portland, Oregon. Her most recent book is *Talk Dirty to Me* (Anchor, 1995).

David Rains Wallace was born in Charlottesville, Virginia, in 1945 and now lives in Berkeley. His most recent book is *The Bone Hunter's Revenge: Dinosaurs and Fate in the Gilded Age* (Houghton Mifflin, 1999).

Peter Booth Wiley was born in Orange, New Jersey, in 1942 and is now a journalist living in San Francisco. His most recent book is *The National Trust Guide to San Francisco* (John Wiley & Sons, 1999). E-mail: pwiley@best.com □